*A Managing Schools Today Legal Guide*

# Pupils, their education
# and the law
## A CASEBOOK APPROACH

**Chris Lowe**

The *Questions* Publishing Company Ltd
Birmingham
1999

Published by
The Questions Publishing Company Ltd
27 Frederick Street, Birmingham B1 3HH

ISBN 1 84190 0060

Edited by Diane Parkin
Designed by Al Stewart
Illustrations by Phil Elliott
Set in 10/14pt Garamond

# Contents

# List of cases

# Documents and circulars

## CHAPTER ONE

# Admissions

## Legal background

NEW interim guidance on school admissions was issued in September 1998, in **Circular 12/98 School Admissions: Interim Guidance**. A new statutory admissions code of practice will be issued in 1999.

The admission authorities for schools are usually Local Education Authorities (LEAs), unless the Instruments and Articles of Government prescribe that the governing body of the school is the admission authority.

The admission authority must publish the admission arrangements each year. These must bear in mind equal opportunities legislation, and must not discriminate against an applicant because he or she does not live in the LEA area.

Each school has a standard number for each relevant age-group. This represents the minimum number of pupils that must be admitted if sufficient applications are received. A higher limit can be set following consultation, and in the case of voluntary aided schools, with the agreement of the Secretary of State.

## New guidance

The new guidance aims to 'balance the rights of parents to exercise a meaningful preference with the need for sensitive but necessary planning of places'.

Parental preference is to be maximised, but since some disappointment is inevitable there must also be clear and adequate information given to parents, and a fair and independent mechanism for resolving disputes.

New independent adjudicators and new independent appeal processes will be put in place. In addition, local cooperation and local forums will be encouraged and will probably be made statutory in the new regulations.

There must be no discrimination against pupils who live outside the LEA, but LEAs are expected to cooperate so that sensible planning can take place.

## Admission criteria

Annex A to the circular contains good practice on admission criteria.

Admission authorities can still operate catchment areas, but no guarantee of places can be given to parents who do not express a preference, as preferences which are expressed must be considered before those who have not expressed a preference.

It is also possible to adopt a system of feeder schools instead of catchment areas.

Schools supported by religious foundations can give preferences to members of a particular faith or denomination, but the details must be fully explained to parents.

Interviews will not be allowed except in the case of church schools where it is necessary to determine the parents' denominational or religious commitment.

As regards infant classes, LEAs must make plans for meeting the Government's pledge to reduce class sizes for five, six and seven year olds to 30 or below by the year 2001. Where extra places are needed these should be in popular and high achieving schools.

Pupils in general should get places in a school near their home. This may mean that in exceptional circumstances the class size limit may be broken.

Academic selection cannot be used for admission to primary schools.

The guidance recommends the practice whereby places are offered to parents in reception classes before their children have reached compulsory school age, and which are accepted and then deferred until the child has reached school age. This must be stated in the admission arrangements.

## Selection

Grammar schools will still continue although parents may petition for a change in the admissions procedure.

Partial selection will only be allowed in the context of fair banding. Schools will not be able to select only those at the top of each band.

Specialist schools may take up to 10% of their pupils according to aptitude.

Problem pupils are not to be weeded out at the admissions stage. Further guidance will be given in the Code of Practice.

## Timing

Deadlines for applications should be common between LEAs of similar size and for similar types of schools.

From September 1999, admission appeals will be conducted independently of the relevant LEA and the school's governing body.

The arrangements will apply to the admission arrangements for September 2000 and onwards.

## Settling disputes

An independent adjudicator from the new panel of adjudicators (see above) will decide on disputes concerning the arrangements.

## Current regulations

If a school is oversubscribed, the LEA and governing body can admit pupils and refuse others according to a published list of criteria, which must not be unreasonable, i.e. criteria which no sensible authority acting with due appreciation of its responsibilities would have decided to adopt.

It follows that schools and LEAs must act lawfully and reasonably when considering applications for places.

Once an offer of a place has been made it is only possible to withdraw the offer in very limited circumstances, i.e. if offered on the basis of a fraudulent or misleading application, or where parents have not responded in a reasonable time. It is not likely to be lawful to withdraw a place once a child has started to attend the school.

An admission authority can, however, refuse to comply with a parental preference for two years following a pupil's permanent exclusion from two or more schools. The parents would not be able to appeal, but the governing body can if the LEA admits the pupil to the school.

## Cases

Admission to schools raises many passions and causes much anxiety. Most of the cases, however, are concerned with the actions of LEAs as the admission authorities, and governing bodies where they are the admission authority. Occasionally heads may fall foul of the system, but usually out of misguided attempts to do their best for disappointed pupils, or to keep unwanted pupils out of the school in defiance of the published criteria. Normally the independent appeal committee puts the matter 'right', but sometimes the issue comes to court as in the **case of the withdrawn offer**.

In **R v Beatrix Potter School ex parte K 1997**, a pupil (K) attending a nursery school was refused admission to the main school, although her brother was already a pupil at the school. The parents' appeal was turned down, but when two other pupils who had been admitted left the school, the head decided to admit K.

In his letter the head stated that all pupils at the school were expected to wear school uniform. As soon as she received the letter the mother bought a uniform, but later that day the head telephoned her to tell her that the offer had been rescinded. The head then wrote to confirm that the offer had been withdrawn, and to apologise for having offered a place. This had been made in error, and the LEA had ordered the head to withdraw it because the Authority did not wish its admission system to appear to be unjust and arbitrary.

The parents applied for judicial review and amongst other things argued that they had expected the offer to be honoured, and had therefore gone out and bought the uniform. Thus they had suffered some personal detriment.

The Court agreed that that there had been a clear promise which the parents had relied on to their detriment.

Sometimes this would be decisive, but in deciding whether the withdrawal of the place was unreasonable the Court also had to consider the LEA's policy which lay behind the head's decision. In addition, the Court had to take into account the speed with which the offer had been withdrawn. In all the circumstances it was impossible to say that the decision was unreasonable, and the application failed.

## Registration and attendance

Once pupils are admitted they must attend regularly and an admission register has to be kept in accordance with the **Pupil Registration Regulations 1995**.

Governors can require the pupils to attend lessons outside the school. They must also allow pupils to attend religious meetings and classes off the school site in certain circumstances.

Schools must maintain an attendance register showing whether absences were authorised or unauthorised.

It must be filled in with ink before the morning and afternoon sessions, and must be kept for a minimum of three years.

Subject to certain restrictions attendance registers may be kept on a computer, but a print-out must be made each month, and a bound volume annually.

## Leave of absence

Pupils cannot be allowed time off school for work during school time except for work experience and any work-related curriculum (see below) organised through the school.

Permission to go on holidays with parents can be granted. It should not be more than two weeks unless there are exceptional circumstances.

Detailed guidance is in the booklet **School Attendance: Policy and Practice on Categorisation of Absence 1994** (available from the DfEE).

## Class sizes

The **School Standards and Framework Act 1998** empowers the Secretary of State to make regulations imposing limits on class sizes for nursery schools during ordinary teaching sessions by a single qualified teacher from the year 2001/2. The duty will be similar to the duty under S14 of the **Education Act 1996** in respect of primary and secondary schools. That is to say that LEAs must make proper attempts to ensure the provision of sufficient nursery education for the children in its area. The courts will not be able to intervene if the LEA makes a proper attempt to comply.

## Implications for management

In their publication of information schools must ensure that the following are included:

- arrangements for any visits by parents to the school;
- details of the admission policy including any places being retained for possible growth;

- details of the number of places available in the previous September and the number of applications for these places, and the number admitted;
- the proportion of places allocated against each admission criterion;
- the number of appeals against non-admission and the proportion which were successful.

Heads and governors should review annually the standard number and the potential entry cohort in future years, and consider whether any change might be necessary in view of the projected figures.

Staff must have clear instructions on what constitutes authorised and unauthorised absence.

Staff must also have clear instructions on the completion of registers. These should be set out at the front of each register.

# Home and school agreements

UNDER the provisions of S110 and S111 of the **School Standards and Framework Act 1998**, the governing body of every maintained school and every CTC and CCTA is required to adopt a home-school agreement and associated parental declaration, which in practice are likely to be combined in one document.

The home-school agreement is a statement of the school's aims and values, its responsibilities to its pupils, and on the other side a statement of the responsibilities of the pupils' parents and what the school expects of the parents.

Governing bodies are required to consult parents of registered pupils before adopting or revising an agreement.

Governing bodies must take all reasonable steps to ensure that all parents sign the parental declaration to indicate that they understand and accept the contents. However, governors are not obliged to get the signature of a parent when they consider that there are special circumstances where this would be inappropriate.

Governors can invite any pupil they consider to have sufficient understanding of the agreement as it relates to him or her, to sign the parental agreement with the parents to indicate acceptance of the school's expectations.

The governing body must have regard to any guidance issued by the Secretary of State and must review the agreement from time to time.

The Secretary of State may prohibit the use of certain forms of words, or words which have a particular effect in home-school agreements.

Breaches of the terms of the agreement will not be actionable through the courts.

Pupils must not be excluded, nor should they or their parents be adversely affected on account of their failure or refusal to sign the agreement.

The governing body or the LEA, if it is the admission authority, must not invite a parent to sign before the child has been admitted to the school; nor make an admission conditional on the signing of the agreement; nor base a decision on admission on whether or not a parent is likely to sign the agreement.

Guidance for schools is contained in the DfEE document, **Home-School Agreements** (ref PPY984).

The guidance covers:

- why the agreements have been introduced;
- how schools can introduce them;
- what agreements should contain;
- what they should not contain;
- what makes for effective agreements.

## Chapter three

# Attendance

Schools have to keep two registers according to the **Pupil Registration Regulations 1995**, one for admissions and one for attendance.

The attendance register must be completed at the start of each morning and afternoon session, showing which pupils are present. It must also show whether the absence of a pupil of compulsory school age was authorised or unauthorised.

Registers are legal documents which can be used in evidence during legal proceedings. Handwritten registers must be completed in ink, but there is an increasing use of computers to keep both registers. Whichever method is used, the original entry and any changes should be clear.

Schools using computers for attendance registers should print out the register at least once a month.

LEAs are responsible for ensuring that pupils of compulsory school age attend regularly. Schools must give the LEA the names and addresses of pupils who have been regularly absent, or have been away for two weeks (except if the absence is covered by a medical note).

All schools have to include rates of authorised and unauthorised absence in their prospectuses and annual reports. Levels of absence are included in local comparative tables which are published annually.

## Leaving date

Each year there is a single leaving date for pupils who have reached the age of 16. The Secretary of State has now chosen the last Friday in June in the school year in which the pupil reaches 16.

## Implications for management

The registers are legal documents and can be used in court proceedings. They must, therefore, be completed consistently by form tutors, and should be checked regularly by line managers.

Teachers must appreciate that registers have to be filled in daily at the beginning of each session in ink. The symbols used, if not laid down by the LEA, should be determined by the school and should be consistently applied.

It is important that the register of authorised and unauthorised absences is completed at the time they become known, since any delay may blur the memory.

Pupils cannot leave school at Easter or the last week in May as used to be the case. The examination pupils can still be granted study leave as before to prepare for the GCSE and other summer external examinations, and these can be counted as authorised absences for registration purposes. The DfEE considers that study leave may not be appropriate for all pupils, and suggests in **Circular 11/97** that schools should consider continuing taught lessons until the end of May and provide a mixture of study leave and supervised revision after that.

**Circular 11/97** also suggests that pupils might be engaged in work experience in their final term as they may now undertake work experience in the last four terms of compulsory schooling. They could also take part in field trips, educational visits, approved sporting activities and link courses. For registration purposes these would all come under the new registration category of approved educational activity, and would not count as authorised absence.

Careful planning needs to have taken place for pupils in Year 11 not taking examinations. It is likely that this planning will have begun a year or so earlier and in nearly all cases will result in individual educational plans. The consultation will involve the school's partners, such as the careers service, educational welfare service, youth service, business partners, and link colleges, in order to fulfil the school's responsibility to ensure that such pupils receive appropriate education.

At the same time schools will have in mind the commitment to ensure that examinations are run efficiently according to the boards' rules. This can be a drain on staff resources, so much so that some schools have felt the need to draw on the services of governors and parents for voluntary supervisory help, or spent money on cover staff. School management at this time of year can be very complex.

## The school day

LEAs determine dates of school terms and holidays. Schools must be open for 380 half days, i.e. 190 days for pupils, except for nursery classes in primary schools.

---

Governing bodies decide the times of sessions. The Secretary of State has merely recommended the following minimum weekly lesson times:

| | |
|---|---|
| Ages 5 – 7 | 21 hours |
| Ages 8 – 11 | 23½ hours |
| Ages 12 – 16 | 24 hours |

These do not include time for collective worship, registration or breaks. Parents must be informed of the times and any changes. Changes to the timings can only be made by the governors after an elaborate procedure. (See **Circular 7/90: Management of the School Day.**)

---

## CHAPTER FOUR

# Curriculum

## Legal background

THE school curriculum for every pupil must be broad and balanced. The Secretary of State, LEAs and governing bodies and heads must all ensure that the curriculum promotes the spiritual, moral, cultural, mental and physical development of all pupils, and prepares them for the opportunities, responsibilities and experiences of adult life.

Every maintained school must ensure that it provides the National Curriculum, religious education, collective worship and sex education (in secondary schools) for all pupils.

The school curriculum can also contain subjects which are not part of the National Curriculum, e.g. personal and social education, or business studies. However, all the courses leading to qualifications must be from the list approved by the Secretary of State.

The National Curriculum comprises nine foundation subjects in primary schools and ten in secondary schools: English (and Welsh in Wales), mathematics, science, design and technology, information technology, history, geography, music, art, physical education, and a modern foreign language (for secondary pupils).

In addition pupils in Years 9 – 11 now have a right to receive careers education.

The core curriculum for 5 – 11 year olds at Key Stage 1 and 2 in maintained schools is: English, mathematics, science, IT, and RE.

## Key Stages

The curriculum is organised in Key Stages depending on age:

|  | Ages | Year Groups |
|---|---|---|
| Key Stage 1 | 5 – 7 | 1 – 2 |
| Key Stage 2 | 7 – 11 | 3 – 6 |
| Key Stage 3 | 11 – 14 | 7 – 9 |
| Key Stage 4 | 14 – 16 | 10 – 11 |

An unofficial Key Stage 5 covers Years 12 and 13, the Sixth Form.

Legally the National Curriculum has to be taught to pupils in the term after their fifth birthday, but if schools admit pupils before then they may choose to teach National Curriculum subjects.

## Programmes of study

At each Key Stage there are programmes of study setting out what has to be taught, and attainment targets denoting the standards pupils are expected to reach.

Geography, history and PE are not sub-divided into different attainment targets. The other subjects are divided as follows:

- English: speaking and listening, reading, writing;
- Welsh: oral (speaking, listening and viewing), reading, writing;
- mathematics: using and applying mathematics, number and algebra,

shape, space and measures;
- science: experimental and investigative science, life process and living things, materials and their properties, physical processes;
- art: investigating and making, knowledge and understanding (in Wales: understanding, making, investigating).
- design and technology: designing, making;
- information technology: capability;
- modern foreign language: listening and responding, speaking, reading and responding, writing;
- music: performing and composing (in Wales: performing, composing, appraising).

## Attainment levels and assessment

In KS1 to KS3 the standard of pupil performance is expressed in levels 1 – 8, with an extra level above level 8 for pupils who show 'exceptional performance'. Pupils climb up the levels as they get older and learn more.

At Key Stage 4 the assessment of pupils is through the Grades A – G at GCSE, with an A* for pupils with outstanding achievements.

By law all pupils should be assessed at four key points in Key Stages 1 – 4. For most pupils this will be at seven, 11, 14 and 16. Some pupils will be accelerated.

At the end of Key Stages 1 – 3 the statutory arrangements for assessment include both teacher assessment and National Curriculum tests. The two have equal weighting, and both must be reported to parents.

The law prohibits schools from offering any course leading to a qualification which has not been approved by the Secretary of State. Circulars of Guidance containing the approved qualifications are sent to all secondary schools.

Schools must report pupils' National Curriculum assessment results to parents and publish a digest of the school's results in prospectuses and governors' annual reports to parents.

Information about assessment arrangements each year are sent to schools by the DfEE and QCA each autumn term.

## Common requirements

In each programme of study it is stressed that provision should be made and emphasis put on access to the curriculum for the great majority of pupils including those with disabilities, the contribution that the subject can make to developing the pupils' ability to express themselves clearly and accurately in English (or if appropriate Welsh), and the need to develop and apply IT in all subjects (except PE).

In Wales pupils should be able to develop and apply their knowledge of the cultural, economic, environmental and linguistic characteristics of Wales.

Although the common requirements are indeed common to all the National Curriculum subjects many teachers under pressure from the mainstream subject requirement do not incorporate them in their teaching.

## Key Stages 1 and 2

From September 1998 to September 2000 schools with KS1 and 2 pupils will continue to be required to teach a broad and balanced curriculum, including all ten national curriculum subjects and religious education.

However, they will have greater freedom to decide what is taught in:

- design and technology;
- history;
- geography;
- art;
- music;
- PE (with the exception of swimming which remains a statutory requirement).

There will be no changes to the existing recording and reporting requirements for these and the other National Curriculum subjects. These are set out annually in the QCA documents **Assessment and Reporting Arrangements: Key Stage 1**, and **Assessment and Reporting Arrangements: Key Stage 2**.

QCA has sent the leaflet **Changes to the National Curriculum in Key Stages**

**1 and 2** to all schools.

Non-statutory schemes of work in science and ICT for use in primary schools have been prepared by the DfEE Standards and Effectiveness Unit and the QCA. Further non-statutory schemes have been prepared in history, geography and design and technology.

## Homework

Following the 1995 Ofsted report on homework in primary and secondary schools and subsequent research, the Government has concluded that homework makes the greatest impact on learning when the homework policy is led by the senior management as part of the school's overall learning strategy, and when tasks are carefully planned and are consistent across the school.

It is also important that parents and pupils are treated as partners and are clear about what is expected.

Pupils should receive prompt and clear feedback on their work and the implementation of the policies should be regularly monitored.

The DfEE issued non-statutory guidelines in November 1998 in the document **Homework: Guidelines for Primary and Secondary Schools** (ref: HGPS S98).

---

The recommended time allocation for homework in primary schools is:

*Years 1 and 2*
1 hour/week (reading, spelling, other literary and number work)

*Years 3 and 4*
1½ hours/week (literacy, numeracy as for Years 1 and 2 with occasional assignments in other subjects)

*Years 5 and 6*
30 mins/day (regular weekly schedule; emphasis on literacy and numeracy but also wider range of subjects)

---

The Government's recommendation of daily reading could be done as part of homework.

---

The recommended allocation for secondary schools is:

| | |
|---|---|
| Years 7 and 8 | 45-90 mins/day |
| Year 9 | 1-2 hours/day |
| Years 10 and 11 | 1½ – 2½ hours/day |
| Years 12 and 13 | this will depend on the individual programmes but guidance should be included in schools' policies |

---

The document points out that various forms of study support are used by schools to complement the setting and assessing of homework, especially where parents were unable to provide appropriate facilities for homework, e.g. homework clubs.

## Sex education

Secondary schools must provide sex education, including teaching about HIV and AIDS and other sexually transmitted diseases.

In primary schools the governors decide whether or not sex education should be part of the curriculum.

Aided and special agreement primary schools are not bound by the detailed arrangements but must keep a statement of their policy.

All sex education must be taught in a way that encourages young people to have regard to moral considerations and the value of family life.

## Withdrawal from sex education lessons

Pupils may not be withdrawn from lessons dealing with the elements of human reproduction and associated physical and emotional changes at adolescence which are contained in the National Curriculum, but pupils can be withdrawn from the non-National Curriculum lessons.

## Health education

All schools teach some kind of health education usually as part of a PSE programme or included in other subjects. Certain parts of drug education, including tobacco, alcohol and illegal drugs are part of the National Curriculum. **Circular 4/89** gives advice on tackling the problem of alcohol misuse.

**Circular 4/95: Drug Prevention and Schools** sets out the statutory position on drug education in schools, and offers guidance on the principles which should underpin drug education.

Drugs education should be part of an integrated health education programme and should:

- give pupils the facts;
- emphasise the benefits of healthy lifestyles;
- make clear the downside and illegal aspects of drugs;
- give pupils the skills to adopt a positive lifestyle and to take a responsible attitude to drugs.

Certain aspects of drugs education are a statutory requirement as part of the National Curriculum. These represent the statutory minimum that heads should ensure are present in their school's curriculum. **Circular 4/95** sets out the position clearly.

## Religious education

All maintained schools must provide religious education for all pupils up to the age of 18, apart from those who are withdrawn.

Most schools follow the locally agreed syllabus drawn up by the Standing Advisory Council on Religious Education (SACRE). These must reflect the fact that the religious traditions in Great Britain are in the main Christian while also taking into account the teachings of the other principal religions.

If a parent asks for a different provision of religious education it is possible for this to be arranged off the school premises.

## Collective worship

Maintained schools must provide daily collective worship for pupils up to 18, unless they have been withdrawn. In county schools it must be wholly or mainly of a broadly Christian character. Exceptions are allowed where the background of the pupils mean that a Christian act of worship is not suitable.

## Case

How the laws and guidance on collective worship and the teaching of religious education should be interpreted came to the attention of the courts in **R v Secretary of State for Education ex parte R and D 1993**, an application for judicial review.

In 1989 parents complained that a primary school did not have daily acts of collective worship which were wholly or mainly of a broadly Christian character, and was in breach of the law.

They also complained that as religious education was taught as part of an integrated curriculum, if they withdrew their children they would be deprived of necessary secular education.

The complaints were rejected by the governing body, and in 1990 the LEA investigated and dismissed the complaints. The parents then complained to the Secretary of State.

The Secretary of State also rejected the complaints, and explained his interpretation of 'worship' and 'collective worship'.

He considered that collective worship should be concerned with reverence or veneration being paid to a being or power regarded as supernatural or divine. This interpretation was challenged in a letter to him by the Parental Alliance for Choice in Education, who asked for clarification of the 'identity of the being that was being revered in the act of worship at the school'. The Secretary of State replied that it was not necessary for him to identify the object of worship so long as one could be reasonably satisfied that there was one.

The applicants contended that the collective worship at the school did not conform to his definition. They also challenged his conclusion that the school conformed to his view that most acts of collective worship should contain some elements which related specifically to the traditions of Christian belief, and in particular accorded special status to Jesus Christ.

The applicants also challenged the Secretary of State's conclusion on the second complaint that there was evidence that a child who was withdrawn from both those elements of religious education provided in the integrated curriculum would be able to participate fully in the secular curriculum. Their counsel argued that although RE was taught separately for one period it was also present in an integrated course for five lessons per week. It was, therefore, wrong for the Secretary of State to argue that they would not be deprived.

The Court held that the Secretary of State had not erred, and refused leave for judicial review.

The judge considered that the Secretary of State had acted reasonably in concluding that the legislation permitted some non-Christian elements in collective worship so long as these did not deprive it of its broadly Christian character.

As regards the second complaint, the judge said a specific request for withdrawal had been made in respect of religious education, but without reference to religious worship. It could not be said that the Secretary of State should have inferred that a request was being made to excuse the boys from religious worship. What the parents were seeking was that during it the boys should not be exposed to non-Christian religious traditions. The withdrawal of the pupils from the school very soon after the request could realistically be regarded as having cancelled the request.

Even so, there was no evidence that the curriculum would result in any interference with a pupil's secular education if he or she were excused from attending religious education.

## Spiritual education

All pupils have to be taught spiritual education as part of their balanced education.

Spiritual education has traditionally been taught through religious education programmes. With the increasing difficulty experienced by some schools in teaching religious education for a reasonable length of time right up to the 18 year olds, other ways of introducing the spiritual dimension have been sought by some schools, and Ofsted inspectors now look to see where the spiritual 'tingle' factor can be detected in the lessons they observe. It may seem to be easier in the arts and literature lessons, but inspectors have let it be known that they have discovered it in many areas of the curriculum.

Schools would be well advised to consider formulating a policy on a whole school approach to spirituality, which is at one with moral, cultural, mental and physical elements of the curriculum to which pupils are entitled.

## Position of heads and teachers

With certain exceptions for teachers in aided and controlled schools, heads and teachers are not obliged to take part in acts of collective worship nor to teach religious education.

In controlled and special agreement schools, 'reserved' teachers for religious education can be appointed.

Heads have a duty to 'make arrangements' for collective worship and to take reasonable steps to find people from outside the school. The head must decide whether any volunteers are suitable.

## Political education

The **Education Act 1996** in S406 requires governing bodies, heads and LEAs to forbid the promotion of partisan political views in the teaching of any school subject, and to forbid the pursuit of partisan political activities by pupils under the age of 12 while in school. Section 407 requires schools to take reasonable steps to ensure that where pupils are engaged in controversial issues they should be offered a balanced presentation.

Anyone who has reason to believe that a school is not complying can complain to the governing body. If dissatisfied with the governors' response they can complain to the LEA (if an LEA school) and ultimately to the Secretary of State.

## Disapplication of the National Curriculum

Heads can disapply or modify the National Curriculum for periods not exceeding six months for pupils who have major difficulties, e.g. medical or family problems, or a SEN pupil who is being assessed prior to the possible issue of a statement of special education needs.

## Careers education and guidance

The **Education Act** gave new duties to governors and heads to work with careers services, to provide them with access to school premises and information on pupils, and to act together to provide pupils with access to careers information.

Although the legislation does not apply to independent schools, the Secretary of State hoped that these schools would consider helpful the guidance offered in **Circular 5/97: Careers Education and Guidance in Schools: Effective Partnerships with Careers Services**.

## Work-related learning at Key Stage 4

The Secretary of State has used his powers under S363 of the **Education Act 1996**, to make regulations to allow schools to set aside aspects of the National Curriculum at Key Stage 4 for individual pupils in order that they can be offered work-related programmes.

The school must meet certain criteria set out in the regulations, and in QCA Guidance, and can then set aside up to two of the following National Curriculum subjects to provide work-related learning opportunities: modern foreign language, design and technology, science.

The programmes should:

- offer experience of the working environment and practices;
- provide pupils with the opportunity to develop literacy, numeracy and key skills;
- complement the National Curriculum education that is being provided in the remainder of the pupil's programme;
- contribute so far as possible towards approved qualifications.

Heads must arrange for the pupils in the programme:

- a careers interview;
- a structured curriculum plan;
- a mentor at the workplace;
- regular liaison meetings;
- to monitor the programme;
- to provide a report for the pupil at least termly;
- to inform QCA by 30 October each year of the proposals for setting aside aspects of the National Curriculum and the number of pupils involved.

## National entry level awards

From September 1998, Entry Level Awards (national qualifications below the level of a GCSE pass, GNVQ Foundation or NVQ level 1) are available for use in schools. Some existing Certificates of Achievement have been amended to ensure that they meet the requirements for National Entry Level Awards. See QCA letter of 19 August 1998, which was sent to all secondary schools. A copy is obtainable from QCA.

## Years 12 and 13

Advanced Level GCE courses are still the mainstay of the Sixth Form curriculum, but increasingly schools are introducing GNVQ courses at intermediate and advanced levels.

The Government has announced changes to 16+ qualifications for implementation in September 2000. QCA has issued guidelines for examination boards. In future the boards will publish 'specifications' for each subject and not syllabuses. Boards are expected to offer five subject options from September 2000

## General National Vocational Qualifications

These qualifications of a vocational nature are now available for use in both Sixth Forms and Years 10 and 11. There are three levels: level 1 or foundation level; level 2 or intermediate level; and level 3 or advanced level. The last two are available in Year 11 and 12.

## Baseline assessment

Maintained primary schools must adopt a baseline assessment scheme which applies to all children on entry to the school. This is for the purpose of assisting future planning of their education. Heads must recommend to the governors a particular scheme chosen from an approved QCA list. If the school is an LEA maintained school the governors must first consider the LEA's own scheme.

## National literacy strategy

All primary schools must have literacy plans in place with literacy targets agreed with the governors. Plans made in Autumn 1998 cover the years 1998 to 2000.

Schools must have a dedicated literacy governor and literacy co-ordinator. Training for heads and teachers is provided.

From September 1998 all primary schools are expected to have 'literacy hours' each day for all pupils. It is not a legal requirement but schools are under pressure to conform or to prove that they have methods that will be equally as beneficial.

The DfEE has published guidance on how literacy is to be taught in those hours.

## Literacy targets

The Government has set a target for 80% of pupils aged 11 to be gaining at least level 4 in KS2 tests by 2002. All LEAs have been given targets which have taken into consideration its historic and current performance. Each LEA has to agree targets for individual schools which take into account the intake of those schools.

Details are contained in **The Implementation of the National Literacy Strategy**, published by the Literacy Task Force.

## National numeracy strategy

From September 1999 all primary schools are expected to have a daily mathematics lesson for all pupils, to include regular oral and mental work.

The head and two other teachers will be able to attend a 3-day training course in the summer term 1999, and a governor will be able to attend for at least one day. Schools will also be expected to devote three Inset days to numeracy, the first being in summer 1999, supported by national training materials.

The Government has set a target of 75% of 11 year olds gaining level 4 by 2002.

## Heads' duties

Heads by virtue of their Conditions of Service are required to 'determine and organise the secular curriculum and ensure that it is followed in the school'. It must be compatible with the governors' policy and with any statutory requirements. The head must also take into account any representations made by the community served by the school and by the chief of police.

## Teachers' duties

Teachers are required by their conditions of service to prepare and plan courses and lessons, including the setting and marking of work, assessing recording and reporting on the development, progress and attainment of pupils.

## Parents' rights

In general parents do not have the right to withdraw their children from the curriculum unless the school agrees.

They do, however, have the right to withdraw their offspring from religious education and assemblies of a religious nature by virtue of S389 of the **Education Act 1996**.

Parents of pupils in maintained schools can also withdraw their children from all or part of sex education, except for the National Curriculum science 'human reproduction and physical and emotional changes of adolescence'.

Parents can also direct any complaints about the curriculum to the governors. The LEA must also have in existence arrangements for considering complaints about the curriculum made to it.

## Equal opportunities

Curriculum planning should ensure that equal opportunities to take part in the whole curriculum are provided for both boys and girls. Pupils with disabilities should also have access to the whole curriculum as far as possible.

The curriculum policy should also promote a multicultural ethos by including multicultural dimensions wherever possible. This is as important in mainly white schools as it is in schools which are rich in multicultural identity.

A practical example of common-sense prevailing in a curriculum issue was reported by the CRE. A Vietnamese boy was allowed by an examination board to take a bilingual dictionary into an examination, but was not allowed extra time for the exam, although other pupils with particular educational needs were allowed an extra 25% of exam time. The examination board said it was working under the rules of a wider joint body and could not depart from the rules. Eventually the head of the joint body advised the local examination board that it could use its discretion to allow the extra time, and also undertook to review the rule, which it has since done.

## Implications for management

It is the head's job to put into practice the National Curriculum determined firstly by the Secretary of State, and then incorporated in the policies of the LEA (if relevant) and the governing body. The allocation of responsibilities for the curriculum is intended to promote the concept of a partnership between the school and the wider community.

In practice it is rare for a chief of police or members of the community, other than parents, to make representations about the curriculum, but if they do heads must not ignore them. They have to be seen to be taking the representations into consideration, although they may decide in the end that they are not acceptable.

A difficulty shared by all schools is fitting all the curriculum requirements into the time available. This is true at all Key Stages but particularly so at KS4. The SCAA (now QCA) booklet **Managing the Curriculum at Key Stage 4** lays out a number of models, but the perfect curriculum does not exist.

At KS4 approximately 60% was recommended by the Dearing Report for the core subjects, distributed as follows:

- English 12½%;
- maths 12½%;
- double science 20%;
- PE 5%;
- RE 5%;
- PSE 5%.

The remaining 40% can be shared between the remaining subjects in a variety of ways.

The national literacy and numeracy strategies should mean that pupils will arrive at secondary schools with higher skills in these areas. This will probably mean that the curriculum at KS3 and then KS4 will need to be re-thought, and teaching methods in some subjects will have to be re-considered, for example in foreign languages and science subjects.

# Raising standards

## Legal background

Following the **School Standards and Framework Act 1998** the Government's thrust is to join LEAs and schools in raising school standards.

LEAs are required to promote 'high standards' in primary and secondary education, and in particular will have to submit 'education development plans' for their area for approval by the Secretary of State.

Both LEAs and schools will have to set targets and will be accountable for meeting them. Schools will in effect have to account annually to the LEA and parents, and periodically through Ofsted inspections.

The 1998 Act also gives a new power to the Secretary of State to exercise general default powers where a LEA is failing to discharge its duties. The Secretary of State may take action if an authority is failing to provide education for pupils at maintained schools 'to an adequate standard'. The Secretary of State will be able to give directions to authorities to ensure satisfactory performance of its duties.

The 1998 Act also puts in place new steps for dealing with schools which are causing concern. Among other things, if the standard of performance of pupils is unacceptably low the LEA may issue a formal warning requiring the governors to take remedial action within a set period. If the school fails to improve, the LEA can appoint additional governors and possibly suspend the school's delegated budget.

The Secretary of State's ultimate sanction is to close the school.

The Secretary of State also puts his faith in the new Education Development Plans which each LEA must draw up in discussion with schools. The plans will set out how the LEA intends to support school improvement to achieve the individual performance targets that each school will set according to the regulations.

All primary schools must carry out baseline tests, and spend more time on literacy and numeracy.

The National Grid for Learning can also be used for finding and using on-line learning and teaching materials. The DfEE has proposed a strategy to help schools keep up-to-date with the development of software and hardware, maintenance and professional development.

Parents are also expected to play a part in raising standards. They will have a written home-school agreement drawn up by the school in consultation with the parents, setting out clearly what the school expects of its pupils and reminding the parents of the importance of attendance by the pupil at the school, discipline and homework.

The complaints procedure, governors' annual report and annual parents' meeting will also contribute to improvement of performance.

## Implications for management

The new provisions replace the failing schools regime introduced in the 1993 Act.

The concept of failing schools covers those 'requiring special measures' to those which are 'causing concern'. Schools which redeem themselves will also be allowed to return to LEA control, instead of remaining in an 'education association', as provided for in the 1993 Act.

## Teaching methods

Schools have flexibility within the National Curriculum to teach the programmes of study in appropriate ways for their pupils' abilities and aptitudes. Teachers can, where necessary, select material from earlier or later stages.

Although it would be true to say that there is no statutory duty laid on teachers to teach in a certain way, strong pressure has been put on primary schools by the Government to have a literacy hour and a numeracy hour each day. The Secretary of State has stated that although it may not be a statutory requirement, schools would have to demonstrate that their alternative methods produced as good a result.

# *Target setting*

## Legal background

One of the main planks of the Government's strategy for raising standards is target setting.

Governing bodies of maintained schools, in compliance with the **School Performance Targets (England) Regulations 1998** made under S19 of the **Education Act 1997**, are required to set targets each year for pupil attainment at the end of Key Stage 2 and in the last year of pupils' compulsory schooling, measured by National Curriculum tests, public examinations and equivalent qualifications.

No additional testing is deemed necessary by the Secretary of State.

Statutory targets had to be set firstly in the autumn of 1998 for performance in the summer term 2000. In September 2000 schools will then have to publish their actual performance against those targets.

In autumn 1999 schools will set targets for 2001. (In the draft guidance it was suggested that schools would have to set targets in 1998 for both 2000 and 2001, but this has been altered.)

In the small minority of schools (mainly middle schools) where a cohort of pupils enters the school just three terms before the end of KS2, targets should be set as soon as possible at the beginning of the school year in which they will take the tests.

In 1999 (the interim year) governing bodies will have to monitor the school's progress towards the targets. They will need to consider what more needs to be done in order to achieve the targets.

LEAs must make Education Development Plans (EDPs) which will include LEA targets. Authorities, therefore, must help schools to set realistic targets, and to agree them.

LEAs are also expected to analyse and disseminate national and local performance data and to provide training.

Guidance on the regulations is provided in the DfEE **Circular 11/98: Target-Setting in Schools**.

## Setting statutory targets

The governing body of schools with KS2 pupils must set targets each year as follows:

- the percentage of pupils who they anticipate will achieve:
  - level 4 or above in National Curriculum tests in English, and
  - level 4 or above in National Curriculum tests in mathematics.

The governing body of a school with KS4 pupils must set targets for those pupils who, on the third Thursday in January in the following school year, will have attained the age of 15 during the 12 month period ending on 31 August immediately preceding that day (the third Thursday in January).

- the percentage who they anticipate will achieve A* – C in five or more subjects in GCSE examinations, equivalent vocational qualifications, or both.

- the percentage who they anticipate will achieve grades A* – G in one or more subjects in GCSE examinations, equivalent vocational qualifications, or both, and the average point score for the school that might be reached by that group of pupils by the end of the following school year in GCSE and vocational qualifications.

The school's performance will be reported each year in the school and college performance tables.

In addition to targets required by the law, governing bodies may wish to set their own targets in other areas.

Infant schools may set targets if they wish, but are not required to do so. Equally, secondary schools can set targets for KS3 cohorts if they wish.

## Reporting targets and performance

Governing bodies are required to publish their targets and achievements in the annual report to parents.

The targets must be published in the annual report each year for four years, including the year in which the target is set.

For the first two years they will appear solely as targets, until that cohort is assessed. In the third and fourth year the targets will be accompanied by actual performance data.

## Exemptions from publication

Whenever there are fewer than ten pupils in the relevant group there is no obligation to publish that target.

## Implications for management

It is the duty of the governing body to set the school's targets. They are not allowed to delegate this responsibility to an individual, but they can delegate it to a sub-committee made up of governors.

The Secretary of State recognises that many schools already set targets. The DfEE is now committed to providing funding and support for the process. Funding will come from the Standards Fund School Effectiveness Grant.

Each autumn term national comparative performance information will be published (including benchmarks). Specific guidance will also be published from time to time in print and on the Internet.

The Secretary of State has also indicated that the arrangements should not become burdensome for teachers. He considers that the administrative load has been kept to a minimum.

Consequently, the requirements refer only to the basics of literacy and numeracy, and the testing required is only that which is already in existence. It is not necessary for any additional testing to be introduced in the school.

Schools will need to determine how they will make the arrangements personal to themselves, and to fit the setting of targets into the normal annual cycle of planning, action, monitoring and evaluation.

The targets set at KS2 will have to be based on the same measure as the national literacy and numeracy targets for 2002, which will have already been agreed with each LEA. Schools must, therefore, agree KS2 targets for 2002 with the LEA. The targets for 2000 will reflect the pursuit of the 2002 aims.

Schools will need to consider whether to set additional targets. If so, then the DfEE would expect that these additional targets would be in support of the general school improvement aims.

Any additional targets might be particularly relevant for special needs pupils, or pupils with high ability. The DfEE expects to provide additional guidance on these matters.

Governing bodies cannot change targets once set, but they will review progress the following autumn and can decide to take additional action if necessary.

Heads will need to consider the school's current practice of reviewing pupils' progress to see whether it fits in with the new cycle.

The school management in conjunction with the governors will need to plan how the governing body will be enabled to fulfil its duties. It is likely that the governors will require the head to provide adequate historical information on past school rolls and performance. Other information, such as the PANDAs, national and local performance tables, and LEA information will be useful sources. Any information about the particular cohort that can be gleaned from previous years will obviously be important, as will subject teachers' estimates of progress.

Heads of schools with KS2 pupils will also need to advise the governing body on what information is likely to be useful in coming to a decision about future attainment in literacy and numeracy. Will information and gradings be required from teachers of all subjects?

Decisions at KS2 and KS4 cannot be taken without subject teachers giving precise information about individual pupils, and making predictions about individual pupils that can then be aggregated in an estimate for the whole cohort. Only in this way will the process be precise and meaningful. The whole staff should have an opportunity to discuss the implications and to share ideas on how best to proceed.

Heads on behalf of governing bodies will have to agree targets with their LEAs. LEAs cannot impose targets but they can suggest appropriate percentages. If LEAs and governing bodies cannot agree targets, LEAs can record two figures in the draft EDP sent to the Secretary of State for approval.

Schools will also have to consider how best to publish these particular performance predictions so that they do not unduly overshadow the celebration of all the other achievements by the school and individual pupils in other fields. Experience tells us that this statutory academic information is eagerly seized on by many parents in order to compare schools, but this should not prevent schools from continually proclaiming the importance of other achievements. Small schools have special difficulties in that a small variation in a small cohort can look massive in percentage terms. This has to be painstakingly explained in the governors' annual report to parents.

There is nothing to prevent the school from publishing other targets and information and providing a commentary on the targets and performance, which may draw attention to contextual information, such as the number of absences, or the number of pupils who had left, or the number who had been disapplied from the National Curriculum requirements.

The DfEE recognises, too, that special schools will also find it difficult to set meaningful targets, but they will have to do so. In the future the findings of the research into appropriate means of measuring achievement at levels 1, 2 and 3 and below level 1, might mean changes when the arrangements are reviewed in 1999.

These new arrangements will have an effect on the new staff appraisal arrangements which are due to come into force in September 1999. Ministers have already announced that appraisal will be more firmly linked to other policies designed to raise pupil achievement. Target setting will be integrated into the appraisal process. Schools will need to consider, therefore, what changes might be necessary in their local schemes, and make allowance for staff training in 1998 and 1999.

## Guidance and information

*The Implementation of the National Literacy Strategy* 1997 DfEE
*The National Literacy Strategy, Framework for Teaching* 1998 DfEE
*The Implementation of the National Numeracy Strategy* 1998 DfEE
*Numeracy Matters* 1998 DfEE
*Careers Education in Schools: Provision for Years 9-11* DfEE **Circular 5/98**
*Better Choices* series ED/DFE 1994 – 1997
*Qualifying for Success* QCA

*Skills for Choice* SCAA (now QCA)

*Learning from Careers Education and Guidance* QCA

*Learning from Work Experience* QCA

*Guidance on the Inspection of Primary/of Secondary/of Special Schools* Ofsted

*Disapplication of the National Curriculum at KS4* 1998 QCA

*Maintaining Breadth and Balance at KS1 and 2* 1998 QCA

*Target-setting in Schools* DfEE **Circular 11/98**

*Taking Forward Our Plans to Raise Standards for All* 1998 DfEE

*Key Stage 4 Curriculum in Action*

*Education for Citizenship and the Teaching of Democracy in Schools* 1998 DfEE and QCA

## CHAPTER FIVE

# Special educational needs

## Legal background

PUPILS have special educational needs if they have learning difficulties. They have learning difficulties if they have greater learning difficulties than the majority of children their age, or disabilities that hinder them from making full use of educational facilities.

Governing bodies must make appropriate provision for pupils with special educational needs. The 'responsible person', i.e. the head or appropriate governor, must make known those needs to all who teach pupils with special educational needs. In so doing they must have regard for the Code of Practice on the identification and assessment of special educational needs

They must also ensure that SEN pupils join in activities with non-SEN pupils as far as possible. The governors must also report annually to parents their policy for pupils with special educational needs.

The governors, in cooperation with the head, must determine the SEN policy and provision. The policy must be published and be readily available to parents. Schools may decide to distribute copies of the policy to parents.

The **Special Needs (Information) Regulations 1994** prescribe the issues which the policies must address.

Guidance is contained in **Circular 6/94: The Organisation of Special Educational Provision**.

The head is then responsible for the day-to-day management of special educational needs.

The SEN co-ordinator or SEN team is responsible for the day-to-day operation of the policy.

LEAs are responsible for drawing up statements of special educational needs for those pupils who are adjudged to require them. Governing bodies, heads, parents and SENCOs have joint responsibility for ensuring that the appropriate provision is made.

## Implications for management

The governors must draw up a SEN policy with the head. They must also decide between them whether the head or a governor will be nominated as the 'responsible person' for special educational needs.

The policy must cover basic information about the aims and arrangements, the allocation of provision, staff development.

Depending on the size and circumstances of the school the head will determine whether to entrust the operation of the policy to a coordinator or to a team.

All teaching and non-teaching staff should be involved in the development of the policy, be aware of the policy and be clear about their responsibilities in the implementation of the policy.

Schools must ensure that statemented children receive the provision stated, and that non-statemented pupils who might have just missed being statemented have their needs met.

Most of the hundreds of cases heard each year by the Special Educational Needs Tribunal (SENT) concern the processes and provision by LEAs. Occasionally cases are against schools.

Many of the complaints heard by the Tribunal involve allegations of delay by LEAs. The **1993 Education Act** included provisions for speeding up the procedure for drawing up and reviewing the statements.

In 1989 a mother complained to the ombudsman (before SENT had started work) that delays had meant her son having to spend longer in a school where he was having particular difficulties.

The ombudsman discovered that the completion of the reports was left mainly to the professional judgements of officers without a time limit being imposed by the LEA. Because of the newness of an educational psychologist, the head's call for an urgent review was unanswered. It appears that no written reports were shown to the mother for years. On the other hand she had attended frequent meetings. The ombudsman decided that the delay in contacting the mother amounted to maladministration, but the absence of written reports should not automatically be seen as such.

It was suggested that the LEA should make an ex-gratia payment and an apology.

## CHAPTER SIX

# Responsibility for the welfare of children

## Legal background

EVERYONE with parental responsibility has a right to participate in major decisions about a child's education.

Parents, even if they divorce, share their rights and duties throughout a child's life. Parents have the right to make decisions and choices, even about how their child is to be educated, subject to other legislation. It is only lost on adoption of the child.

If parents were not married at the time of the birth only the mother has automatic responsibility, but fathers not married to the mother of the child can acquire parental responsibility by agreement with the mother or a court order, or by becoming the legal guardian.

The LEA has responsibility if named in a care order.

Schools must treat all those with parental responsibility equally, including special educational needs assessments, receiving reports and invitations to parent evenings.

## The Children Act 1989

The Act defines 'children in need' as those who are unlikely to achieve a reasonable standard of health or development without the provision of services, and those with disabilities. It requires teachers and social workers to work together with the aim of preventing problems for children as well as finding a cure for problems. Schools are entitled to ask for help for children in need, and local authorities should have counselling and social cultural or recreational facilities that can be called on.

The Act emphasises that the child's welfare is paramount, that delay in taking action should be avoided, that children's own wishes should be taken into account, and that parents have continuous responsibility.

Schools are expected to work with a wide range of agencies. Clear aims, clear roles and joint training were envisaged by the Act. The paper **Working Together Under the Children Act 1989** recommended, among other things, that schools should identify a designated teacher for children in need. This could be the head or a senior member of staff.

Schools need to know:

- who has parental responsibility?
- to whom should reports be sent?
- what is an 'at risk' register?
- what orders concerning pupils are in existence (e.g. residence order, education supervision order, child assessment order)?

## Employment of children

Heads need to be aware of the legislation concerning the employment of children, and to take note of local by-laws.

These are currently under review although legislation which came into force in August 1998 will require changes. Local authorities have the power to review their current by-laws and update them to include a list of jobs which children aged 13 and over may do, and to set out the restrictions on children's working hours during school days, Saturdays and holidays. Work on Sundays is still limited to two hours, and children under the age of 14 cannot be employed before 7 am and 7 pm, even for delivering newspapers, for more than five hours per week for under 15s, and eight hours per week for over 15s.

A model has been provided, but local councils are free to make their own decisions within the limits set.

In the regulations and model, children (anyone not over compulsory school age) must have at least two weeks free from work during the school holidays.

## Guidance and advice to pupils

Teachers are required to provide guidance and advice to pupils on educational and social matters and on future education and careers.

## Information about pupils

Heads have to ensure that a written report is sent at least annually to parents. If sent only once it must contain a minimum of specified information laid down in the **Individual Pupils' Achievements Information Regulations** which are updated from time to time.

Teachers have to contribute to the reports, but the format is largely up to the school as long as it contains the minimum information.

If a pupil moves to another school the head must provide the receiving school with a report.

All leavers are entitled to a leaving report on their examination results and other achievements, which currently is in the format of the National Record of Achievement (NRA). It has to be signed and dated by a teacher who knows the pupil.

## Progress file

Since 1991 pupils have been entitled to receive, as well as reports, a NRA, which records a summary of their educational achievements. This will eventually be replaced by a progress file which will be a slimmed down version, fulfilling much the same purpose.

Teachers have a duty to supply information for the file, which will belong to the pupil, and must be available to the pupil and his or her parents, but not the public.

## Recording and reporting

As part of their duty of care teachers are required by their conditions of employment to keep records on pupils' progress and achievements, of discussions between them, of aspirations and problems. Much of this information will then be reported periodically.

Teachers must keep a record for each pupil, to include their academic achievements, general progress and other skills and abilities. Schools may also require teachers to keep other records, which are not required by law.

Parents, and pupils over 16, can have access to these records free of charge.

A pupil's UCAS or job reference, if kept semi-permanently on a computer, must be made available to a pupil or parent. If not on computer they can remain confidential if the school wishes. This may cease to be the case in the future.

Information about SEN pupils is covered by other regulations.

## Consulting with parents

Consulting with parents is another part of a teacher's professional duty. While many can take this in their stride for some it appears full of pitfalls. Teachers can face hostility and abuse, can be accused of discrimination, or lack of sensitivity.

This can lead to complaints being made by parents to heads or sometimes governors, and occasionally the LEA.

Heads need to recognise that this is an area where teachers may require support, but do not recognise or admit it.

Heads and senior staff need to have in place training procedures and support processes that will enable them to deal with both the teachers' and the parents' problems with understanding and sensitivity.

Ultimately all parties are working for the pupils' best interests, but at times some parties need to be reminded of this, before entrenched positions are taken up.

The handling of teacher-parent relationships comes mainly from the head's and senior teachers' well of experience.

## Receiving examination results

Pupils receiving their external examination results are almost invariably at their most up-tight. Most schools make meticulous arrangements for discreet handing over of the results, and have counselling on hand for those who need it.

Imagine what it must be like to be given the wrong results.

This is what happened to a college student in 1964. She applied for a post as a dispenser's assistant at a hospital and was asked to let them know the results of her four GCE subjects when she received them. She received a letter indicating that she had passed all four subjects and told the hospital and her friends.

When the certificate had not arrived six months later she made enquiries and was told that there was no certificate because she had failed all four subjects.

She sued the city council and the college principal on the grounds that the shock had made her ill and that she had lost the opportunity of re-sitting the papers in the autumn.

The principal offered to let her continue her studies at the college with special coaching and without fees, but as she was now studying other subjects she declined.

In the County Court the principal said she was an average student who had had great difficulty with a two year full-time course and would have had great difficulty with a part-time one. He would not have advised her to return to college. He did agree that the news would have been a shock to her.

The council pointed out that she had been allowed to keep her hospital post and that she was, therefore, better off as the hospital would not normally have employed a person without GCE passes.

The Court accepted that it was unlikely that she would have returned to sit the examinations as the Court now knew that in three subjects she had gained only the lowest grade. The judge was, however, convinced that she had suffered nervous shock and awarded damages. **Hollands v Canterbury City Council and Hooke 1966**.

## Child abuse

The **Children Act 1989** provides that LEAs must assist local authority social services acting on behalf of children in need, or enquiring into child abuse. LEA schools, GM schools, CTCs, FE and Sixth Form Colleges under an extension by the Secretary of State, are also subject to the provisions. Every school must, therefore, have a child protection policy and procedures to be followed.

**Circular 10/95: Protecting Children from Abuse** gives guidance.

## Implications for management

Teachers should be taught to recognise the signs of possible abuse.

It is not uncommon for teachers to suspect that a pupil has suffered some abuse outside school. Sometimes there are visible signs, bruises and scratches. Sometimes it is the child's behaviour or emotional state which give the signals.

Although teachers might seek further information they should not do so beyond that set out in the school's procedures.

The head or another senior member of staff should be designated to liaise with the social services department and other agencies, and all other teachers should know who the designated teacher is.

Where the designated teacher is not the head there must be clear guidelines as to how the head is to be kept informed.

Although it is usually the designated teacher who will make day-to-day decisions about investigations, it is ultimately the head's responsibility to determine whether to investigate the matter further, and what kind of action to take. This is because if the school decides to hand the case over to the social services for further investigation, parental high dudgeon invariably follows.

This is what happened in **R v East Sussex CC ex parte R 1991**. A head was suspicious of bruises discovered on a six year old's thigh. He informed social services. The mother was interviewed by a police officer and clamed that she had hit the child with a wooden spoon because he had been naughty.

This was corroborated by the child.

Social services decided to hold a child protection case conference and informed the mother's solicitor. The mother's request to attend was turned down but she was allowed to put her views in writing.

On the morning of the conference the social worker tried in vain to contact the mother to see if she had any more she wanted said on her behalf. The decision of the conference was that the boy and his sister would be put on the child protection register.

The mother applied for judicial review of the decision. She contended that the decision was unfair because she had not been able to attend the conference and to make proper representations. She further claimed that the decision was an unreasonable response to what was no more than ordinary disciplining of a naughty child by a parent.

The Court rejected her claims, holding that she had had a reasonable opportunity to state her case, and that although the injuries to the boy were not serious there was cause for concern. The school and local authority had shown that they were trying to help, not criticise. Their attitude was not unreasonable.

Anyone who has attended such conferences knows the agonising that can take place and the concern expressed for the welfare of the child. Sometimes the combined wisdom is not sufficient and mistakes are made, but more often than not the decisions reached are sensible and sensitive.

The requirement to inform the welfare services of any concerns a school may have about the welfare of a pupil, and possible abuse, can naturally lead to parental backlash. There is sometimes a fine line between abuse and acceptable chastisement. Schools try to be sensitive in the handling of the issues, but on many occasions complaints are made to governors or LEAs about a school's allegedly unwarranted interference.

In one such case a parent complained to a local government ombudsman about how a local council had dealt with the concerns of a third party regarding her daughter's welfare.

The daughter was a pupil at a special school. The school considered that she had both learning and behavioural problems. A class teacher reported to one of the senior teachers that a voluntary helper at the school, who was a neighbour of the girl and her parents, was concerned about the girl's welfare.

He had seen her locked out of the house and crying in distress, and had gone to the house to ask the father to let her back in. Other incidents had also occurred which caused the neighbour concern.

The senior teacher decided not to make an immediate request to the social services department. She did, however, ask the neighbour to monitor the situation and also tackled the mother about possible problems with the child at home. The mother denied that there were any.

Eventually, matters turned worse and the class teacher informed the senior teacher that the mother was constantly turning up late with the child, and openly chastising the child in front of teachers and other pupils.

When confronted the mother continued to deny the problem and decided to take the child away from the school, after claiming that another child had sexually interfered with her daughter. She complained that the school had done nothing about it.

The senior teacher now contacted the Education Welfare Service (EWS) and discussed her concerns. The EWS interviewed the neighbour who intimated that another neighbour was also worried. The EWS asked for the other neighbour to contact them. This second neighbour let the EWS know that she had no such concerns, and furthermore complained that the voluntary helper had divulged confidential information about the alleged sexual abuse. This second neighbour told the mother what was going on. When she heard about this the mother complained to the ombudsman through a solicitor.

The ombudsman found that the senior teacher had acted reasonably in informing the EWS. It was not unreasonable, as claimed, because the girl was still on the school's roll even though she had been withdrawn. It was also appropriate for the voluntary helper to contribute his concerns. On the other hand it was inappropriate for him to be asked to contact a neighbour who he believed shared his concerns.

It was a matter for grave concern that a voluntary helper should have such confidential information, which she had divulged to a neighbour.

The ombudsman recommended that the council should apologise formally for the distress caused through the way that she had learned of the council's concern about her daughter. She should also be paid £150.

This amounted to maladministration because the council allowed enquiries of a sensitive nature to go outside its control. The enquiries should have been made by an appropriate officer. **Complaint against Newcastle upon Tyne City Council 1998**.

## Allegations against staff

It is quite common for children to make allegations of sexual or physical abuse against teachers. Obviously any such allegation has to be taken seriously, even when as so often happens, the accusation has no substance.

The school must have clear procedures for handling these incidents. The procedures must be in line with the local Area Child Protection Committee procedures. Guidance produced by the teacher unions is set out in **Circular 10/95**.

# Bullying

Bullying is defined in **Circular 10/95** as deliberately hurtful behaviour repeated over time where it is difficult for those being bullied to defend themselves.

Schools would be well advised to have anti-bullying policies and it is vital that they should act quickly and decisively to combat it. This is not only in the precise and immediate interests of the pupil being bullied, but also because a lack of immediate action is now being interpreted as a sign of negligence by the school and is giving rise to a number of cases. Sometimes the cases may be taken by way of complaints to governing bodies or LEAs and sometimes to the courts.

If a school fails to take action against a bully once the bullying has come to its attention then an action for negligence might lie against it, if a pupil has suffered either physically or emotionally.

In particular, a court would look to see whether adequate supervision was in place at break times and in between classes.

The anti-harassment measures in the **Criminal Justice Act 1997** have already led to a 14 year old boy being found guilty of bullying a 13 year old boy, who in the aftermath of the bullying had tried to hang himself.

The attacker was given a conditional discharge by a youth court and ordered to pay his victim £10 compensation. (*The Times* 13 October 1998.)

In a civil case a university student who suffered from cerebral palsy claimed damages from Nottinghamshire CC for a breach of the duty of care by Bolsover School, where she had been a pupil six years earlier. She alleged that she had been bullied for more than a year by members of the school's steel band in which she played. She said that they had made determined efforts to exclude her and instituted whispering campaigns to make her life miserable. The bullying had drastically affected her confidence, and had almost ruined her university career.

The judge said that bullying required an appropriate response from teachers, but in this case the evidence was only of minor complaints with mentions of looks and atmosphere. The school had not acted improperly in the way it had dealt with the problem.

The judge was critical of her father, a teacher at another school and a former governor at Bolsover School, for his attempts to deal with his daughter's claims of bullying. The judge felt that the parent was in a good position to deal with the situation and to decide what was in the girl's best interests. He could think of nothing more upsetting than six years of complaints procedures and litigation. (*The Times* 16 July 1994).

In another case an 11 year old boy, whose statement of special educational needs referred to his emotional vulnerability, was injured by a pellet fired from a gun by a 13 year old pupil but brought onto the site by another pupil. The head in the first instance excluded the two boys for a fixed term, and later changed this to permanent exclusion.

The victim suffered adverse psychological effects, and was terrified of meeting the boys who had been responsible. His father wrote to the governors indicating clearly the damaging effect that a return to school by the perpetrators would cause.

When the governors met to consider reinstatement they questioned the two malefactors and their parents but not the victim or his parents.

The boy who shot the pellet argued that the victim had accidentally got in the way of the shot. The committee was convinced by the boy's demeanour and the fact that the other witnesses' evidence was unreliable. It decided to reinstate the two boys.

The victim's father sought judicial review of the decisions arguing that undue attention had been paid by the respondents to the interests of the two boys' previous good record rather than to the effect that their decision would have on his son, the victim. The governors should have had more regard for the welfare of other children at the school.

The judge dismissed the application, holding that the governors had taken reasonable steps to inform themselves of all the circumstances, and had given proper consideration not only to what had happened but also to the future if the two boys were reinstated.

The applicant appealed, and the Court of Appeal overturned the previous decision. The Court decided that the governors' inquiry was flawed, as the investigation of the incident itself and the investigation of the probable effect on the victim were inadequate.

The Court ordered the case to be sent back for redetermination by a differently constituted committee of the governing body and a different LEA representative. **R v London Borough of Camden and the Governors of the Hampstead School 1996.**

## CHAPTER SEVEN

# Health and safety of pupils

## Legal background

LEAs, governing bodies, heads and teachers all have statutory and common law duties to ensure that schools are healthy, safe and secure, for pupils as well as employees. The Health and Safety Executive, the Government's watchdog agency, takes an interest in schools as it does any other institution.

The **Health and Safety at Work Act 1974** is mainly concerned with employees but it also covers pupils, who in this context are 'visitors'. Their health and safety must be ensured as far as is 'reasonably practicable'.

The many regulations that have emanated from this Act and from European Commission directives have made the duties much more precise.

## Implications for management

LEAs and schools must first of all have health and safety policies, known to everyone who works at the school and regularly reviewed. Each school should also have a health and safety representative, and most will have health and safety committees too. Regular risk assessments will also be carried out, which can be initiated by the head, the governors, the health and safety committee or representative, or by an outside person, such as an officer of the LEA.

Ultimately it is everyone's duty to be vigilant and to report any defects in premises or equipment.

It is necessary for everyone, including pupils, to recognise that they have a responsibility. The part that pupils can play will depend on their age and aptitude, but many schools involve pupils actively in the review process through school councils. Some schools also have a practice of highlighting one safety aspect in morning assemblies.

Pupils are particularly concerned to be involved in the security aspect following the various horrendous assaults and killings that have taken place in schools. The Government has provided funding to improve school security, but even though this may have improved matters, schools must have procedures to review constantly the working of those measures, as it is only too easy for them to lapse or be misused in time.

It is important for the head and governors in their risk assessments to ensure that there is a procedure known to everyone for checking and controlling visitors to the premises, and procedures for dealing with intruders.

In particular the pupils themselves should be regularly informed about aspects of the policies and procedures. They should also recognise the part that they could play in keeping the school safe and secure by reporting possible problems, and avoiding dangerous areas, or acting responsibly in potentially dangerous areas.

When a teacher takes on a duty, whether voluntarily or as directed by the head, he or she must perform that duty conscientiously and to the best of his or her ability, bearing in mind the nature of the duty and the tasks laid down by the management. It is the responsibility of the head to ensure that the duties and tasks are necessary, and not unnecessarily onerous. Consultation with staff and a sharing of the duties load are important in ensuring that the safety system works properly.

## Negligence

Despite all the best efforts accidents will still happen and as soon as they do, someone will undoubtedly be considering whether something could have been done to prevent them, and whether there is any legal liability.

When considering whether an injury is accidental or due to negligence a court will ask:

- was a duty owed to the plaintiff by the defendant?
- did the defendant discharge that duty properly, or not?
- did the plaintiff suffer any damage because of the defendant's actions?

For there to be any negligence the answer must be 'yes' to all of these.

In other words, it is perfectly normal to feel conscience-stricken when an accident happens, but for someone to be liable for damages the law requires that on the balance of probability someone was negligent, i.e. did not do something he or she ought to have done, or did something he or she should not have done. In 1954 a very learned judge, Mr Justice McNair, summed up the dilemma when he remarked in **Jeffery v London CC 1953**, that a balance must be found between meticulously supervising pupils every moment they are at school and encouraging sturdy independence as they grow up.

In order to gain compensation for an injury at school it is necessary for it to have been caused by someone's negligence. In other countries such occurrences are covered by insurance and there is virtually an automatic pay-out. Not so here, unless parents have themselves insured their offspring against injury. Some injuries might be so severe that they result in potential future expense and/or loss of earnings. It is not surprising that pupils and their parents try to obtain payments for damages. Such cases seem to be on the increase.

In some cases, insurance companies of LEAs and schools have settled out of court without prejudice, arguing that in the long run this is a cheaper option.

Courts have on the whole been more realistic than sympathetic. They have recognised that it is not possible to watch every child every minute of the day. On the other hand they have been hard on those who have given little thought to the proper discharge of their duties.

In determining whether there was reasonable care shown, courts will apply the test of what was 'reasonably foreseeable'. They will judge whether a teacher or school authority could in all the circumstances have reasonably foreseen the consequences of a particular course of action or lack of action.

## In loco parentis

In a classic definition of a teacher's duty of care, Mr Justice Cave in **Williams v Eady 1893** said that: "The schoolmaster is bound to take such care of his boys as a careful father would take of his boys."

In this case some boys in a preparatory school broke into a conservatory and were injured by phosphorous which they found in a bottle. The Court held the school liable. The judge considered that it was evidently negligent to leave a bottle of phosphorous lying around in a place accessible to boys, 'knowing what boys are'.

However, not many parents are in charge of 30 or so children who change every hour, and in 1968 Mr Justice Lane considered that the notion of the duty of a teacher needed to be extended to take account of the kind of incident which might happen in a large secondary school. He suggested that the head's duty, bearing in mind the known propensities of boys and girls between the ages of 11 and 17, was to take all reasonable and proper steps to prevent children in his care from suffering injury.

He felt that in the case he was hearing the school fell short of these high standards. Some boys found a discarded piece of trampette elastic during a protracted mid-morning break. They used it as a catapult to project one of their mates across the loggia. The elastic broke or flew out of the hand of one of them and destroyed the eyesight of another pupil.

The judge found that it was negligent to leave a piece of elastic in an open wastepaper basket. There was a possibility that some physical damage might occur.

The judge also considered that the standard of supervision did not measure up to the high standard required. There were only two teachers with four prefects, four sub-prefects and four monitors. It may have been that on that one day insufficient staff were available to supervise. If the system had worked then one of the staff or prefects would have seen what was going on, it would have been stopped in a relatively short time and the tragic accident would have been averted. **Beaumont v Surrey CC 1968**.

In another case a five year old boy climbed onto the glass roof of a lavatory after school. He fell through and died from his injuries. The parent maintained that if an adult had been present the accident would not have happened. He argued that a supervisor should have been present until all the children had left the school.

The judge said that the school had thought it necessary in the case of children under five to have a supervisor until the children were collected, but had not thought it necessary in the case of five year olds, and that was a decision taken by a responsible person. The judge considered that it would require strong evidence to convince him that it was wrong. The case was dismissed.

## Playground duty

Playground duty is perhaps the bane, but a necessary one, of teachers' professional lives. All sorts of accidents can occur and do, usually when the duty teacher is at the other end of his or her beat.

What is important is that a system of supervision should be in being, should be known by the staff, who in turn should conscientiously carry out the duty. When these things happen the courts will find it hard to decide that negligence has occurred, although there are some narrow shaves.

This was what happened in **Ward v Hertfordshire CC 1970**. An eight year old pupil, while racing across a school playground before school opened at 8.55 am, stumbled, crashed into a wall and was seriously injured.

In the High Court the judge held that the local authority as the employers and also occupiers of the school premises were in breach of their common law duty to take reasonable care for the safety of the children. The judge said that in his view a prudent parent of a large family would have realised that the playground with its wall of jagged flint was inherently dangerous.

Therefore, some supervision was necessary, not necessarily continuous, but from time to time, controlling any risky activity.

The Court of Appeal unanimously reversed the ruling. Lord Denning said that a third of the village had similar walls and so had 16 schools in the county and, "goodness knows how many in the country at large. But this does not make them dangerous."

The Court also took note of the head's statement that even if he had been in the playground he would not have stopped the children playing. Racing between the walls had continually gone on during all the time he was there and no harm had come of it.

Lord Justice Salmon said: "I dare say that a small boy had occasionally fallen and scraped his knees . . . and hurt himself to some extent. But this is the sort of thing that happens in playgrounds. It would be wrong to try to protect them against minor injuries by forbidding the ordinary pleasures which children enjoy." He could not see why, even if a master had been present, the master should have prevented the children from racing as the boy was doing when he met with the accident.

He went on to say that if the accident had been caused by children fighting or indulging in some dangerous game which a master should have stopped if he had been there, the fact that there was no supervision might have given rise to a good cause of action. But on this occasion the Court considered the absence of a supervisor to be irrelevant.

A similar decision was reached in the leading **case of the playground slide**. One frosty morning before school officially opened, a young pupil was playing on a playground slide on the ice with friends when his feet slipped and he received severe injuries to his head. Even five years after the accident his speech remained slurred and walking was difficult for him.

When the accident happened the duty teacher was in the staffroom on the other side of the school. Three weeks previously Essex CC had directed that a teacher had to be on duty in the playground for 15 minutes before school began (and also at the end of school). However, the directive had not been delivered to the boy's school. The school playground was habitually opened at 8 am and it was normal for children to gather there for at least half an hour before school began.

The parents claimed that the playground should have been supervised, that the supervisor should have stopped the sliding and that the surface should have been treated.

The judge considered that the matter of supervision was a grey area. But the judge did not consider that the parents had a right to impose a responsibility on teachers outside the ordinary school hours. He did not consider that the head was negligent in allowing the pupils to be within the comparative safety of the school. He also took into account the head's request that parents should not send their children to school unreasonably early. He saw the opening of the gates as an act of grace, not as an acceptance of responsibility.

The judge also dismissed the parents' contention that the sliding should have been stopped. The judge expressed his incredulity at the suggestion. He thought that if a school authority would seriously declare that sliding on ice is a dangerous game, he would feel obliged to declare on his part that the children of this country are free to slide on ice in a sensible and orderly manner whenever an opportunity arose, which they and their elders have been doing for centuries. "There is nothing with which a child cannot hurt itself and no game which may not develop into unruly conduct." In this case there was no evidence that there was any disorder. "Life is full of dangers which children must learn to recognise and develop the ability to avoid."

The parents also argued that as the playground surface was treated the day following the accident it should have been the practice beforehand. The judge thought instead that it was simply a natural reaction to the unfortunate event.

All in all the judge concluded that it was a genuine accident. **Mays v Essex CC 1975**.

## Midday supervision

The reasonableness of a school's arrangements for the safety of pupils during the midday break was considered in **Nwabudike v Southwark London Borough Council 1996**.

A primary school pupil absconded during the lunch break and was knocked down by a car. He claimed damages from the council for negligence. The Court turned down the claim. The pupil had been determined to leave the site against the school rules, and had deliberately avoided the physical barriers on the path which were designed to warn pupils of the danger.

There had been only one similar incident in the preceding six years, and the Court did not consider that the school had been in breach of its duty of care here. The judge considered, as many previous judges had done, that there had to be a balance between a child's safety and a siege mentality. The school on the evidence seemed to have done all that could be reasonably expected to ensure pupils' safety.

## Accidents in PE and games lessons

Accidents are more likely to occur in areas where there are dangerous activities, such as science laboratories or workshops or gymnasia or sports fields.

Where there is specialist equipment only those teachers who are trained in the handling of that equipment should be allowed to use it. And only those who are trained to play and coach potentially dangerous games should be allowed to teach them.

Trained teachers of rugby football will know the rules about binding in the scrum, or the dangers of the 'Fosbury flop' and so on.

Specialist teachers will be trained to deal with all normal occurrences. Sometimes, however, the practices in a particular school will be outside a teacher's experience. It will be a matter for the teacher's judgement whether to change the practice or accept that the school's approved practice has stood the test of time.

In the **vaulting case**, a teacher set up four different exercises in different parts of the gymnasium. The teacher demonstrated to one group how to steady fellow pupils jumping over a vaulting box. When satisfied that they knew what they were doing the teacher moved to other groups and while he was supervising them, away from the vaulting group, one boy fell as he jumped over the vaulting box.

The Court investigated whether the supervision of the teacher was a reasonable PE teacher practice and whether it accorded with the normal accepted practice in the school. The Court discovered that it was and indeed was a practice that had been safely used for many years. The teacher had not been negligent, nor had the school and LEA. **Wright v Cheshire CC 1952**.

However, in another vaulting case, **Gibbs v Barking Corporation 1936**, a teacher was held not to have taken reasonable care when a boy fell while vaulting without a competent person standing by the box ready to support the jumper.

## Out-of-school activities

Out of school activities and school visits are subject to the same rigorous rules about health and safety, and since the environments may be less familiar to the staff and pupils, will require even more careful planning.

Attention should be paid to:

- safety on the journeys, at the venues, in residential accommodation;
- fire hazards;
- supervision ratios;
- emergency arrangements (including communication);
- preparation of pupils;
- staff training.

For all off-site activities a risk assessment should be carried out, covering:

- what risks are known?
- what might be assumed?
- who is affected?
- what safety measures need to be in place to reduce the risks to acceptable levels?
- can the group leader guarantee that these measures will be provided?
- what steps will be taken in an emergency?

The DfEE has issued guidance on **Pupil Health and Safety on School Visits** which supersedes **Circular 22/94: Safety in Outdoor Activity Centres**.

## Qualifications

It is important that teachers taking games where specialist knowledge of health and safety issues is required, over and above the ordinary knowledge of a teacher, should have that knowledge. Normally PE teachers will be qualified, but sometimes they have to gain further qualifications in new areas. For example, they may need to take a course in teaching trampolining or one of the martial arts.

## Excuse notes

PE teachers often have to deal with suspicious excuse notes. Sometimes they are clearly forgeries, sometimes not. It is a matter of judgement whether to accept them or not. It would be helpful to the PE department if they were supported by a clear school policy on this, one that is known both to staff and parents (and pupils too). It is often wiser to accept the note at the time and then follow it up afterwards to ascertain whether it is genuine.

The reason for this is illustrated by the **case of the keen but disabled pupil, Moore v Hampshire CC 1982**.

A girl with a congenital hip defect was injured while attempting to do a handstand. Her mother had written to the school explicitly stating that the girl should not do any kind of PE or games. The mother had also met the head to stress the girl's incapacity. It was subsequently noted in the girl's records.

However, the girl herself was very enthusiastic about doing PE. She told the head of PE on one occasion that she would soon be able to participate, and then later turned up with PE kit, persuading the PE teacher to let her take part. It was then that she injured her ankle.

The girl should have been given more adequate instructions about the handstand activity because she had just joined the class. The teacher should also have supervised her more closely as he knew of her condition.

The Court decided that the teacher did not come up to the high standard of care required of a specialist in that area. He should have told the child that he had to check with the mother whether she could participate, especially as the teacher had prior knowledge of the girl's wish to take part.

When a parent clearly directs the school about a medical condition, this must be followed by the school until the parent equally clearly lifts the restriction. This would normally be done in writing.

Also, if a pupil with a known disability is accepted into a PE class, he or she should be supervised closely.

## Drugs education

See the section on Health Education (p.20).

## Pupils with medical needs

**Circular 14/96: Supporting Pupils with Medical Needs in Schools** summarises the main legal provisions, recommends that schools draw up policies and procedures, and suggests health care plans, which include medication arrangements, for pupils with medical needs.

In general parents are responsible for their children's medication. The head is responsible for deciding whether the school can assist a pupil who needs medication. School staff should not as a general rule administer medication without receiving appropriate information and/or training.

The **Medicines Act 1968** places restrictions on dealings with medicines. Anyone administering a medicinal product by injection must be qualified, although swift action taken by a member of staff in an emergency is acceptable.

The **School Premises Regulations 1996** require all schools to have accommodation for medical treatment and care of pupils.

## Implications for management

Unqualified teachers should not be asked to cover PE lessons where the activities require special knowledge. It is reasonable, however, for an unqualified teacher to cover for absent PE staff if they know the degree of control that is necessary and know the basic rules and practices of the game. They must, of course, exercise ordinary reasonable care.

There is nothing wrong with non-PE trained staff refereeing or supervising a game, since most amateur referees are from non-PE trained walks of life. They will, however, have received some training these days in what the job of a referee entails.

It is important for the school to have a policy on this, and to ensure that cover staff are fully briefed by the teacher in charge of PE before the lesson.

In the **referee case** a referee of a rugby match involving 18 year olds which took place out of school did not apply the rules regarding scrummaging. As a result a 17 year old was severely injured. The referee was found to have breached the duty of care owed to the players by not applying the rules laid down for under 19 matches. **Nolan v Smolden 1996**.

## Other specialist areas

In addition to PE teachers other teachers of specialist subjects, such as science, and teachers of craft subjects owe an even higher duty of care than others because of their extra specialist training. These days teachers in these areas receive health and safety training and have to attend periodic refresher courses. This has not always been so.

In **Noonan v ILEA 1974**, a boy filled a syringe with sulphuric acid from an unlabelled beaker in a science laboratory while the teacher was out of the room. He squirted it at another boy and scarred him permanently.

It was alleged that the LEA was negligent in leaving unlabelled dangerous chemicals on a bench. The teacher claimed that he had issued a warning to the class not to touch anything, but this was denied by the boy who had caused the accident. He said that he thought the liquid was water.

The judge awarded damages, holding that even if a warning was given, a much more graphic and specific warning should have been given as the substance was so dangerous.

The failure to label the liquid and to give an adequate warning constituted a departure from the high standard of care.

## Outside the school gates

The question of the responsibility of school staff for the safety of pupils once they have left the school site has concerned many schools.

The **Teachers' Pay and Conditions Document** includes in a teacher's contractual duties the safeguarding of pupils' safety 'when they are authorised to be on the school premises, and when they are engaged in authorised activities elsewhere'.

Teacher unions are adamant that heads do not have the power to direct teachers to supervise pupils outside the school gate after the school day has ended. It would be in the head's power to direct staff to keep the pupils on the school premises while waiting for transport or parents at the end of the day. If this went beyond the (say) 15 minutes, which is likely to have been the time set aside for after-school duties, then there would be a case for adding this extra supervision time to the 1,265 directed hours.

## After school

Teachers have generally accepted the need to supervise pupils as they leave school. At times they feel that their goodwill is being exploited, particularly where bus duty is included.

At one school staff had watched pupils onto buses at the end of the day for many years, even though the buses lined up outside the gates. Since there was only the width of the pavement between the exit and the buses, and no crossing of the road was necessary, they did not find the task too onerous. Then, as part of a road-widening scheme a lay-by was constructed on the other side of the road.

The staff decided that they could not accept the responsibility for seeing the pupils, aged 11 to 16, across the road. The head and governors supported this stance. The LEA responded that the general responsibility for health and safety of the pupils lay with the governors, and specifically with the head as part of her conditions of employment. The LEA cited the fact that the headteacher's conditions of employment contained the duty to maintain good order and discipline at all times during the school day, when pupils are on the premises or engaged in authorised activities elsewhere.

The LEA claimed that the lay-by was a much safer place to pick up the pupils and that only a few vehicles used the road at the time the pupils were crossing the road. They further claimed that the staff had supervised pupils for years and no substantial extra burden was being asked of them.

The head's riposte was that it was precisely because she was ultimately responsible for safe practices that she could not accept responsibility for the new position where 300 pupils were leaving the premises to walk home and a further 300 were crossing the road to catch buses. The staff were prepared to see that the pupils left the school in an orderly fashion, but neither she nor they would accept responsibility for the crossing of the road.

The LEA considered this unreasonable and confirmed that the teachers were covered by the LEA insurance in the event of a claim for negligence. They thought that it was not any more burdensome for teachers to stand in the middle of the road while children crossed than to walk up and down the pavement keeping pupils in order.

The head clinched the argument by pointing out that the teachers had no legal right to hold up traffic on the road.

At this point the parents heard of the LEA's proposed arrangements and protested in large numbers.

The compromise was that the Authority provided a crossing patrol and the school cooperated by ensuring that the pupils left in good order, and in manageable groups.

Teachers have in any case a common law duty, as well as a contractual one, to ensure the safety of pupils at all times. If a teacher sees pupils misbehaving outside the school as he or she is leaving, he or she cannot ignore the incident and must intervene. A teacher may also voluntarily offer to supervise pupils while waiting for the school buses outside the school gates, and must also act with the same vigilance as at other times of the day.

In both instances the teacher will be on duty and will be acting in the course of their employment. Therefore the employer (LEA or governing body as relevant) will be vicariously responsible. And although the teacher also has a personal liability, this is no greater than if an accident occurs in a classroom.

The question of whether a school should have employed a supervisor at the end of the school day to supervise pupils as they left the school was considered by the Court of Appeal in **Wilson v Sacred Heart RC School 1997**.

A boy was injured in the eye when he was struck by a coat which another child had swung like a lasso. He claimed the school had been negligent in not supervising the passage from the school door to the school gate. If an adult had been on duty supervising the departure from school, the boy who swung the coat would not have done so.

The High Court found for the boy, holding the governors liable for negligence, but the Court of Appeal disagreed. There was evidence that care assistants were on duty during the lunch hour, but no need had ever arisen to suggest that supervision at home time was necessary. The head pointed out that at lunchtime over 90 pupils were in the hall at any one time and over 100 pupils in the playground for more than an hour at lunchtime. The need for supervision at lunchtime was therefore self-evident and was provided.

The Court viewed the very short time during which pupils left the school at the end of the day as a quite different situation, even though it was accepted that the pupils could be in a boisterous mood.

There was no evidence to suggest that supervision from the school door to the gate was standard practice, nor that it was necessary, and the claim for damages for personal injuries was dismissed.

## Negligence of pupils

Sometimes it is the pupils themselves who are negligent rather than those whose job it is to supervise them.

Usually it is the school which deals with such instances under its disciplinary procedures. A number of cases have got as far as the courts.

In the **hand-drier case**, a 15 year old boy was given permission to leave a chemistry lesson to go to the toilet after spilling some concentrated sulphuric acid on his hand. The teacher did not know that he had taken a phial of the acid with him. He claimed later that he wanted to test its reaction on toilet paper.

Before he had completed his experiment he heard footsteps and in panic poured the acid down the tube of a hot air drier. Before he could return to remove the acid another boy had used the drier with the result that some of the acid splashed on his face causing a permanent scar. The culprit was charged with assault occasioning actual bodily harm.

The magistrates found that he knew he had created a dangerous situation but found him not guilty on the grounds that he had not intended to harm anyone.

The prosecution appealed on a point of law. The Court of Appeal was asked whether the magistrates had properly considered whether the boy had been 'reckless' of the results of his actions.

The Court held that as the magistrates had found as a fact that the defendant understood what he had done, the inescapable inference was that the boy had either decided to take the risk of someone using the drier before he could make it harmless, or had given no thought to that risk. On either of these counts the boy should have been convicted.

The Court remitted the case to the magistrates with a direction to convict. **DPP v Khan 1989**.

## Negligent provision of education

A relatively new phenomenon is the rise of actions for damages for negligent educational advice and teaching.

In 1995 five cases of alleged negligence were heard together by the House of Lords, involving LEA officers and advisers, schools, and social service departments. At this time the Court was asked simply to rule whether in each case the authorities could have a legal liability if the facts could be proved. The Court decided that it was possible for schools and LEAs to be sued for negligence if they are careless in carrying out their responsibilities.

In one of the cases, the **Hampshire case**, it was alleged that the head of a primary school had been negligent in failing to refer a child for formal assessment of his special educational needs, or to an experienced education psychologist. It was also alleged that the advisory service was negligent in failing to ascertain specific learning difficulties and failing to advise the parent properly. The parents complained that it had taken ten years before a statement was drawn up and provision made.

The question asked of the Court was whether a head and advisers are under a duty to pupils to exercise skill and care in advising on educational needs. Their Lordships held that since education is the very purpose for which a pupil goes to school, a head, being responsible for the school, must have a duty of care to exercise reasonable skills. A head cannot reasonably ignore the underperformance of a pupil which had been drawn to his or her attention. Similarly in the case of an adviser.

However, they were only bound to exercise the skill and care of a reasonable head and adviser, not the skills of an education psychologist.

The parents were allowed to take their case to trial.

In the **Pamela Phelps case**, a 23 year old mother was awarded damages of over £40,000 against an LEA which had failed to diagnose her dyslexia.

She was an intelligent woman but with a reading age of seven when she left school in Hillingdon at 16. She was dismissed from her first job because she made too many mistakes, and this was followed by a series of menial jobs. At the time of the hearing she had a reading age of 10½.

The judge held that the educational psychologist had made errors in diagnosis when she concluded that Pamela's problems were emotional. He considered that the errors in diagnosis were more than errors in judgement but a failure to exercise the degree of care and skill expected of an ordinarily competent educational psychologist. She should have looked further into the girl's problems and did not.
The judgement included the names of a further seven special needs teachers

or psychologists, who at one time or another assessed her. One had assessed her IQ in her infant school as 93, which he said was well within the national average band. At her next school her head of year had reported that she lacked motivation and did not try. Her mother said that she knew something was wrong but no-one would listen.

However, in November 1998 the Court of Appeal overturned this judgement on the grounds that the educational psychologist had not voluntarily assumed responsibility for any damage caused by her misdiagnosis, and did not have a duty of care towards Ms Phelps unless she had assumed such a responsibility. The psychologist's duty was to advise the school and LEA. It is a matter of public policy that an LEA cannot be held liable for exercising its statutory duty to make decisions when assessing a pupil's special educational needs.

The case will now be heard by the House of Lords. **Pamela Phelps v London Borough of Hillingdon 1998**.

In another case concerning dyslexia (**Rhiannon Anderton v Clwyd CC 1998**) a High Court judge had ordered the county council (and therefore the school) to release within 42 days a full set of records relating to the education of the applicant, who had left one of the county council's schools in 1990.

The applicant was alleged to be dyslexic and contended that she had a cause of action against the council because the head of the school had failed to recognise her dyslexia, or to refer her to a specialist.

The judge decided that the medical evidence offered in support of the application disclosed that the applicant had suffered a personal injury, but subsequently the Court of Appeal held that the medical evidence fell far short of establishing that Ms Anderton had suffered any psychiatric injury. Although personal injuries include statutorily any impairment of a person's physical or mental condition. The Appeal judges said that even if dyslexia could be regarded as an impairment it was certainly not caused by the defendant. It was a congenital condition and disclosure of school documents would not affect it one way or another. The Court of Appeal accordingly allowed the appeal and set aside the order for disclosure of the documents.

## Implications for management

Although these cases involved special needs, it is likely that allegations of negligence could be made about other aspects of education.

The Lords' ruling makes it clear that for a public authority such as an LEA or school to be liable for negligence in the exercise of a discretion conferred by statute, it would need to be shown that the decision was altogether outside the ambit of the discretion.

But if a decision has been taken to implement a particular course of action then the negligent implementation of that decision could be open to question.

Because the test to be used is that of the ordinary competent person exercising that skill, it will be difficult for plaintiffs to prove negligence. However, the Phelps case shows that it is possible for a court to deduce that the degree of skill and care used was not up to the standard of the ordinary member of the profession.

As in other negligence cases the employer will be liable for any negligence by an employee unless the employee acted outside his or her contract and conditions of service.

## CHAPTER EIGHT

# Equal opportunities

## Legal background

IN accordance with the provisions of the **Sex Discrimination**, **Race Discrimination** and **Disability Discrimination Acts**, if a girl is treated less favourably than a boy, or vice versa, potential problems can occur in such areas as admission, curriculum provision, extra-curricular activities and discipline.

The Equal Opportunities Commission believes that there are still problems. Some teachers have different expectations of boys and girls. Boys too often receive more teacher attention. Boys tend to dominate the use of science and design and information technology equipment and girls are often subjected to verbal and sometimes physical abuse by boys.

## Implications for management

Schools have an obligation to strive to provide an environment which is free from sex, race and disability discrimination. They should actively promote the concept.

It is important the head (and senior management team) should constantly review the working of the equal opportunities policy, and to promote it in the staff training programme.

All schools should have an equal opportunities policy and a designated member of staff with the responsibility for monitoring equal opportunities issues. Consideration of these issues should appear regularly in management meetings, though these may not always be explicit.

One area that has given cause for concern is the question of school uniform.

In a leading case of **Mandla v Dowell Lee 1983**, the House of Lords ruled that a head's refusal to admit a Sikh boy to his private school unless he removed his turban and cut his hair was unlawful racial discrimination. Both the County Court and the Court of Appeal had held that the rule was justified in terms of the purposes of a school uniform, and that Sikhs were not a racial group as defined in the **Race Relations Act 1976**. The boy could have complied with the rule.

The House of Lords reversed the decision. The Lords held that the phrase 'can comply' covered customs and cultural norms as well as physical possibility. The 'no turbans' rule could not be justified on educational grounds and the Sikhs, they ruled, were an ethnic group.

This has meant that in the context of school admissions and exclusions, dress regulations, which result in the rejection of a pupil who cannot comply with them for cultural or religious reasons, are likely to be unlawful.

Since then courts have ruled that Gypsies are a racial group and Rastafarians do not constitute a distinct ethnic group.

A rule which lays down a different standard of dress for boys than girls will come under scrutiny. Some schools forbid girls to wear trousers, for example. Other schools forbid boys to wear jewellery but permit girls to do so. If the school wishes to preserve this stance then to successfully defend a charge of discrimination the school will need to draw up a dress code for both boys and girls showing even-handedness. A rule for girls might prohibit the wearing of trousers, while the code for boys might forbid the wearing of earrings.

It was established in a non-educational case, **Smith v Safeway plc 1997**, that it was not necessary to have the same code for both men and women. A court will look at the overall intention and effect of the code.

Another area of concern has been the number of pupils from ethnic minorities who were being excluded from school. A number of surveys have been carried out, the first one by the CRE in Birmingham in 1979. The investigation showed that ethnic minority pupils were four times more likely to be suspended than white pupils for similar offences.

The CRE has often said that teachers are rarely overtly discriminatory. More often it is unconscious and unintended. Often discrimination is the result of applying requirements which have an indirectly discriminatory effect. Consequently it is possible that discrimination in education is more rather than less extensive than other areas.

Heads have to be sure that both they and colleagues are scrupulously fair in applying school rules and criteria for exclusion. There is no place for indirect prejudice nor stereotyping in the decision-making process. The aim is to ensure equality of treatment.

## CHAPTER NINE

# Discipline and behaviour

SECTIONS 60-68 of the **School Standards and Framework Act 1998** now contain provisions relating to school discipline, most of which are not yet in force.

The responsibilities of governing bodies and heads are now contained in S61 of the **School Standards and Framework Act 1998**.

A series of six circulars in 1994 gave guidance on changes in the law concerning pupils presenting particular difficulties. In general their advice is still relevant to the amended 1998 provisions.

The circulars point to inconsistencies between schools in the use of sanctions, particularly exclusion, and suggest that schools should do all that is reasonably possible to avoid excluding pupils.

It remains, however, the LEA's ultimate duty to intervene if there is a breakdown of discipline. But schools must be responsible for the conduct and behaviour of pupils and set the standards required.

Following the 1998 Act, maintained school and city technology college governors will be required at a date to be determined to adopt 'home-school' agreements, explaining the respective responsibilities of school and parents, and setting out what is expected of the pupils.

Exclusions are included in sections 64-68. Parents of excluded pupils will be allowed to address the governing body before any decision is made to confirm, or not, a head's decision to exclude.

There is no longer any mention in the 1998 Act of the need for exclusion appeal panels to take into account the interests of other pupils and members of staff when making a decision.

## Implications for management

### Discipline policies – governors

Governing bodies must have a written statement of general principles for an overall behaviour and discipline policy, which must be reviewed periodically. Policies should include:

- the ethos of the school, its values, and the boundaries of acceptable behaviour;
- the school's moral code;
- positive and constructive rules of conduct;
- the rewards and punishments to be fairly and consistently applied.

They must consult the head and parents and take into account their views before finalising the statement.

The governors can also determine that particular disciplinary measures can be established by the head and give guidance as appropriate. This advice might cover:

- bullying;
- sexual harassment;
- establishing and maintaining good attendance and preventing unauthorised absence.

They must also ensure that the school follows policies to promote good behaviour and discipline.

The head still has responsibility for the day-to-day maintenance of discipline but the governing body is expected to satisfy itself about the policies that the head puts into practice.

### Discipline policies – heads

The head must draw up the discipline policy, setting out measures to:

- promote self-discipline and proper regard for authority;
- encourage good behaviour and respect for others;
- ensure pupils' standards of behaviour are acceptable;
- regulate pupils' conduct.

Heads must publicise the policy to parents and within the school, and at least once a year bring it to the attention of pupils, parents and members of staff.

Heads must only act in accordance with the policies and criteria laid down by legislation and the governors. They must ensure that staff and pupils know the standard of behaviour required and the sanctions that are allowed in the school. Often the reminders to staff and pupils will be by 'drip-feed' through bulletins or in assemblies, which will reinforce the policies contained in staff handbooks and prospectuses.

## Punishment

The general principles for inflicting punishments in schools were laid down nearly 100 years ago in **Mansell v Griffin 1908**. The judge said that any punishment must be moderate, not dictated by bad motive, and be a normal punishment within the school.

## Jurisdiction of the school

Heads and teachers are often called upon to deal with incidents involving their pupils which happen to and from school. Complaints about misbehaviour at lunchtimes in shopping precincts and on school buses figure prominently. Schools usually accept some responsibility out of concern for the school's image and the moral and social development of their pupils.

On the other hand heads are also apprehensive about the lack of support they sometimes get from parents and others when they do take action.

The legal basis for punishing pupils for misdemeanours committed off-site and outside school hours were set out as long ago as 1893 in **Cleary v Booth**.

On the way to school two pupils, Booth and Callaway, met another from the same school, Godding. Callaway assaulted Godding but the head, Mr Cleary, caned both Booth and Callaway. The head was convicted of assault on Booth by a magistrates court on the grounds that he was not entitled to punish a pupil for an act which took place off the school site.

As this was an unprecedented case it was sent to the High Court. One appeal judge pointed out that a teacher is in loco parentis, so that authority is delegated by the parent to the head who has responsibility for discipline and organisation and for bringing up children in habits of good manners and consideration for others. It cannot be that it is only on the school premises that a head has to ensure that they are well-mannered.

Another judge in support said that it is in accordance with ancient practice that a parent may delegate the right to inflict reasonable chastisement to a schoolmaster. It will be a question of fact whether the master is right in inflicting punishment. Since the master is entrusted with the moral training of pupils, such a duty cannot cease as soon as the pupil leaves the school site, especially as the opportunity to exhibit moral conduct comes better when outside the school than while under the eye of a teacher.

Authority delegated to the school is not confined to the school site, or when pupils are engaged in formal activities off-site, but it is also understood that parents can take back their authority. They must do this formally so that the head is quite clear about the extent of the withdrawal from the school's jurisdiction. Then other considerations may enter, such as any home-school agreement which may have been reached, and whether by their actions the parents have effectively withdrawn their child from the school. Decisions on these can only be made on the facts of each case.

## Detention

Legal authority for putting pupils (including Year 12 and 13 pupils) into detention are now contained in the **Education Act 1997**.

Schools have statutory authority to detain pupils after school on disciplinary grounds, without the consent of the parent.

However, heads must first of all let all parents (including parents of pupils admitted part way through the year), pupils and staff know that detention will be used as a sanction in appropriate circumstances.

The detention must be given either by the head or any member of staff to whom the head has delegated authority to detain pupils.

The detention must be 'reasonable'. What is reasonable will depend on the facts, but the legal definition goes something like this: the action taken must be such that any person in possession of all the facts would consider it to be reasonable.

Heads are required to be reasonable in the period of notice to be given to parents – they must also give parents 24 hours' written notice of the detention, telling the parent that the pupil will be detained, where and when, and for how long. This allows the parent to make any representations.

Schools must also take into account whether the parent can reasonably make suitable arrangements to get the child home after the detention.

## Whole class detention

The changes in the regulations will probably not affect the question of keeping whole classes back in detention, regardless of who is guilty and who is innocent. Detention must still be 'reasonable'.

In **Terrington v Lancashire CC 1986**, Mr Terrington claimed damages for the false imprisonment of his son who had been kept in detention with the rest of his class for some ten minutes after school.

The registrar who heard the case found that although there had been false imprisonment the council had proved that it was justified.

He accepted that good teaching practice sometimes demanded blanket punishment of a whole class.

Mr Terrington appealed to the County Court. He claimed that he had verbally and in writing withdrawn his consent for his son to be detained for minor indiscipline, and also that the punishment was not reasonable, because his son had not been involved in the incidents which led up to the detention. Detaining the whole class was unreasonable.

In dismissing the appeal the judge said that although punishment should not be indiscriminate, and blanket detention should only be used as a last resort, in certain cases it could be reasonable to hold a whole class responsible.

He was not convinced that the pupil had not been involved in the indiscipline, and there was no evidence that the father had in fact withdrawn his consent for detaining his son. The letter referred to was in effect only a protest at this form of punishment.

However, the judge made clear that if there had been such evidence then the claim for false imprisonment would have succeeded.

## Implications for management

The new law removes the possibility of a parent claiming that the school has falsely imprisoned his or her child, but the statutory discretion does not give schools an unqualified right to detain pupils. Detentions must be a reasonable and proportionate response to the offence, and schools are obliged to take account of any special circumstances about individual pupils, such as their age, any special needs, religious requirements and whether the parent can get the child home afterwards.

This latter requirement gives a let-out for parents who do not wish to be helpful. It is not open to them just to say that they cannot fetch them, however, since there may be all sorts of ways to transport the child home. Nevertheless, if confronted by an obstreperous parent it will take some time and trouble to show the parent how it can be done. Heads will need to agree a policy on this with the governors, whose support and guidance is likely to be crucial.

Heads will need to consider the extent of their delegation of the authority to detain pupils. Whatever his or her decision, it will be necessary to ensure that all staff know the procedures. It is good practice to have standard letters, but schools differ in their practice of informing parents; some use pupil post, while others post the letters.

It is likely that two days will have to be left between the giving of a detention and the actual detaining in order to give parents their statutory right to make representations about it.

Parents do not, however, have the right to refuse to allow the detention.

Governing bodies should review the school's arrangements for detention as part of their consideration of the disciplinary statement.

As far as whole class detentions are concerned, it might be acceptable to detain a class for a few minutes for disciplinary reasons, but if this resulted in pupils missing school buses or previously arranged meetings, it might not be reasonable. Certainly, anything longer than five minutes might reach the realms of the illegal, since innocent pupils will be involved, and innocent children who are falsely detained tend to have parents with short tempers.

The use of detention, as with other forms of punishment used in a school, should be clearly explained in the prospectus and all staff should be aware of the circumstances in which each punishment would normally be used, bearing in mind the need for moderation and reasonableness.

# Exclusion

## Legal background

The provisions concerning exclusions are now contained in the **Education Act 1996** as amended by the 1997 Act and the **Standards and Framework Act 1998**.

Detailed arrangements for exclusions are set out in each school's Articles of Government. They are slightly different for LEA, GM and aided schools.

There are two types of exclusion – fixed and permanent. Fixed terms cannot exceed 45 days in any one school year.

Only the head can exclude, and having done so must inform the parents of the pupil (or the pupil if over 18) that the pupil has been excluded, the length and reasons for it. The head must also inform the parties that they have the right to make representations to the governors and the LEA. If the exclusion is permanent there is also a right to formally appeal to the LEA who will refer it to a special Appeals Tribunal.

Following the 1998 Act, parents will eventually be allowed to address the governing body before a decision is made to confirm the exclusion. This provision is not yet in force.

The governing body has the right to direct that a pupil excluded for a fixed or permanent period should be re-admitted. The LEA can also do this but must first consult the governors.

The governors have a right to appeal against an LEA's decision to reinstate a permanently excluded pupil. The parent (or pupil if over 18) has a similar right of appeal. The appeals will be heard by the local Appeal Panel.

All disciplinary decisions and appeal hearings must accord with the principles of natural justice, i.e. the pupil must be allowed to state his or her side of the case; neither the head nor anyone else who has previously been involved in the disciplinary issue should be present when the appeal panel makes its decision. Heads and others can, however, be called as witnesses to the panel hearing, but must withdraw at decision-making time.

The decisions of the appeal committee and the grounds on which it was made must be communicated in writing to the parents (or pupil if 18+), the LEA and the governing body.

The head must comply with the direction, but if the LEA and governors disagree about the date for reinstatement, the head must take the pupil back at the earlier date.

There are strict time limits for the decision-making (see **Circular 10/94**).

The funding of excluded pupils follows the pupil who has been permanently excluded, and will be transferred to the new school (see **Circular 17/94**).

## Discouraging schools from excluding poor performers

The Government has proposed changes to the method of calculating performance tables to discourage schools from permanently excluding poor performers in the run up to GCSE examinations.

Any 15 year old who is excluded from a maintained school between 1 September and the January census date will count on the excluding school's roll for the performance tables.

## Exclusion from two or more schools

The 1998 Act repeats the 1997 Act's provision that a school is not obliged to admit a pupil under the parental preference rules if the pupil has been excluded permanently from two or more schools. There is no parental appeal in these circumstances. However, the admission authority can direct that the pupil should be admitted to a particular school. The governors can appeal against this within 15 days.

## Cases

Most of the parental challenges to schools' decisions to exclude concern the procedures used by the school.

An important case of exclusion, **R v London Borough of Camden and the Governors of the Hampstead School ex parte H**, is set out in the section on bullying above.

In **R v The Governors of St Gregory's RC Aided High School 1994**, the parents of a pupil sought a judicial review of the circumstances of the permanent exclusion of their son, with a view to the decision being quashed.

Following an incident in which the pupil was alleged to have told a teacher to 'f**k off', the pupil was first excluded indefinitely and then permanently by the head when the boy denied his part in the incident. The parents appealed against both exclusions and claimed that their son was not a liar.

The governors' committee did not allow the pupil or the boy's mother to speak at their first hearing, and this was according to the Court a clear flaw. However, the governors made it clear that they would have allowed reinstatement if the boy had apologised, even though the parents thought it was just the alleged swearing that had triggered the exclusion.

The parents appealed. The committee heard directly from the pupil but did not permit either of his parents to be present, and also did not receive first hand evidence of the incident. However, it was clear from the committee's minutes that they had considered whether the boy had done what he was accused of doing and whether the exclusion was appropriate. The committee had also sensed a certain tension between the parties and so decided to hear from the applicant in the absence of all the other parties – head and parents.

The High Court decided that if the totality of the proceedings was considered, the errors in procedure were not fatally flawed. The committee had conducted a full review of the evidence obtained by the head, and had allowed the applicant to be heard. There was good reason to believe that the applicant and his father fully understood what transpires at the hearing, and that the father had considered that the hearing was fair, but was dissatisfied with the result.

The Court then looked at the question of the head's reasonableness in making the exclusion. They reiterated the Wednesbury approach to 'reasonableness'. The Court is not concerned with a function of review or appeal, but is concerned with the question of whether or not the decision was 'so absurd that no sensible person could ever dream that it lay within the power of the authority so to act'. **Associated Picture Houses Ltd v Wednesbury Corporation 1948**.

The Court concluded that the applicant had not established that the head was unreasonable in the decision he had reached. The application failed.

This flexible approach to procedures in exclusion cases was repeated in a 1998 case.

A seven year old SEN pupil who had been statemented was permanently excluded from his school for misbehaviour, which was upheld by the governing body and appeal committee. A judicial review of the decision was sought and the judge held that the appeal committee was wrong in not giving a proper statement of its reasons for concluding that the child had been rightly excluded. However, he also held that the error was not sufficient to undermine the decision, and the chairman's later affidavit explaining the factors which had weighed with the committee was sufficient. The judge also considered that the procedures followed had not departed in any material way from those laid down in DfEE **Circular 10/94**, even though he could not accept the county council's argument that the committee was not obliged as a matter of law to have a regard to the guidance. **R v Northamptonshire CC ex parte W 1998**.

On the other hand the procedures were also questioned and found to be wanting in **R v Roman Catholic Schools ex parte S 1998**. A girl pupil was permanently excluded from a Roman Catholic special agreement school for, it was alleged, taking part in a serious assault on a fellow pupil, a boy. The decision was upheld by the governors and appeal committee. A judicial review was sought.

The girl complained that the process used by the school to identify her was faulty. The judge agreed, and also considered that she had not been given a proper opportunity to clear her name. The judge did add, however, that the governors and committee had acted conscientiously and in good faith. He hoped that the risks that are inherent in identifying malefactors would not place an unreasonable burden on those who served voluntarily on such bodies.

One added curiosity in this case was the fact that the police had been called in to investigate the assault, and eventually the girl had been convicted of causing actual bodily harm. Later the conviction was overturned, but none of this was seen to be relevant in the consideration of whether the exclusion had been fair. The head had been barred from interviewing her prior to the exclusion by a condition of her bail, but had otherwise acted fairly, and done all he could in the circumstances.

Another school in Derbyshire was also adjudged to have been in error in its procedures and was ordered to pay £300 to the family of a girl who had been permanently excluded.

The girl and another pupil were expelled after they had viciously punched and kicked another girl. The girl had to be taken to hospital. Both sets of parents appealed. Separate hearings for the two girls were held, but the parents of one girl complained that the hearing had not been conducted properly.

The ombudsman decided that there were a number of procedural faults, including the absence of a clerk and the holding of a hearing in the school. The ombudsman concluded that the defects in the circumstances were sufficiently serious to make the hearing invalid, and ordered compensation.

The head thought that the ombudsman's findings were 'horrendous'. He considered that the attack had been vicious and could have resulted in even more serious consequences. He had decided on permanent exclusion because he wanted to send a clear message that this sort of behaviour was not acceptable. He felt that it was wrong for money to be paid to the attacker, since the lay panel of governors had done their best. (*The Times* 31 October 1996.)

The danger inherent in conducting investigations into disciplinary incidents was also illustrated in **R v Cardinal Newman's School, Birmingham, ex parte S 1997**.

A pupil was accused of attacking another pupil during the lunch break. The classroom assistant who saw the incident did not know the pupil's name, but in the presence of two teachers subsequently chose a photograph which the teachers identified as S.

The head was informed, but not of the circumstances of the identification. The head excluded the pupil permanently, which was upheld by the governors and the appeal committee.

The Court decided that the decision to exclude S was faulty and had to be set aside. Pupils suspected of acts of indiscipline must be given fair opportunities to put their side of the case. Those making decisions, therefore, had to consider the evidence in an even-handed manner. The issue of an identification should always be fully explored. The initial account of the description given by the witnesses should be recorded.

The Court considered that the head had acted with complete propriety, but he had not been fully informed. The governors and the appeal committee had not made sufficient enquiries concerning the identification procedure, and had not given S a chance to put her side of the story.

A head's rationality was also called into question in **R v Solihull Borough Council ex parte W 1997**.

A pupil was permanently excluded for brandishing a knife outside the school site. The pupil argued that he had indeed made a threat but not with a knife. He later admitted that a knife had been involved but not with an open blade.

The head did not believe this story and excluded him. The governors confirmed the exclusion and the LEA's appeal committee rejected his appeal. His parents took umbrage and an application was made for a judicial review challenging the decision, on the grounds that the LEA's decision was irrational.

The High Court did not agree, holding that it was perfectly appropriate for the school and the LEA to decide that wielding a knife was so potentially dangerous as to merit permanent exclusion.

The judge also considered the process used by the head to investigate the incident. The head had considered whether there had been an incident of indiscipline and had concluded that there had been. He next considered the pupil's previous behaviour, his school record, the surrounding circumstances, the safety of other pupils and other relevant factors. This could not be criticised.

The LEA appeals committee had also acted with due propriety in considering whether a different response might have been more appropriate and concluding that it had been a reasonable decision.

The failure to give a parent the opportunity to make representations also resulted in a successful challenge to the exclusion of a pupil in **R v Governing Body of The Rectory School and the London Borough of Richmond ex parte WK 1997.** The school had excluded the applicant for a fixed term of 15 days and later permanently.

The mother questioned the head's earlier decision on the grounds that the maximum of 15 days was too severe. If it had been less than the maximum a

Sometimes parents contribute to the problems that their children are having, and causing, at school. In **R v Neale and Another ex parte S**, the question of whether a school could take into account a mother's behaviour was considered.

A pupil in a Birmingham junior school was excluded on a number of occasions for disruptive behaviour. There was an attempt to agree a contract but nothing came of it. When the head excluded the boy indefinitely, his mother and a representative of the African People's Education Group went to the school and physically thrust the pupil into a classroom. The head called the police, who removed the intruders.

The head then made the exclusion permanent. The governing body invited the mother to their meeting where they were considering whether to uphold the exclusion or direct reinstatement, but refused to admit the representative of the African People's Education Group. The mother then withdrew. The governors upheld the permanent exclusion, and the mother appealed to the LEA.

The LEA decided to direct reinstatement. The governing body then appealed. The appeal committee upheld the LEA's decision, but substituted a later date for reinstatement. The boy returned to school but the provision made for him became a further matter for dispute. The school was closed for several days, the mother claiming that it was because of a strike by the teachers, and the respondents claiming that it was a management decision taken in the interests of safety of pupils and staff, which had been threatened by demonstrations at the school, and the media attention.

The governors asked the Secretary of State to intervene under S68 of the **Education Act 1944**. The chairman also wrote to the mother setting out a series of proposals for a planned return of her son. The proposals were conditional on the pupil's response to the programme of reintegration, and the mother's support. She was given a deadline for a reply but rejected it.

The boy was finally allowed to return to school for the remainder of the summer term to complete his junior school education.

Judicial review was then sought by the applicant to quash the permanent exclusion decision by the head, and the decision of the head and governing body not to comply with the decision of the LEA appeal committee. Declarations were sought that the decisions were illegal. It was also suggested that the decisions might have been indirectly on the grounds of the pupil's and mother's racial origin.

The application was dismissed by the judge. He held that there was no evidence from which it would be right to infer that the respondents were in any way influenced by racial considerations.

The mother's attitude to the head and/or the governors, as expressed in her defiant attitude, must of necessity be relevant when determining that an exclusion should move from indefinite to permanent status.

The governing body was also right in deciding that it did not have to re-admit the pupil until the termination of the appeal process.

The balance of the evidence suggested that the head and governors had made considerable efforts to persuade the mother to use outside agencies to help her son.

In addition, the judge added, even if the applicant had established the grounds upon which relief might be granted, the Court would be bound to hold that relief should not be afforded, as it would achieve no purpose. It would not in any way change the way in which the applicant's further education would take place.

The Court's decision underlines the fact that education is a three-way partnership between school, pupil and parents. It is a legal truth as well as a matter of simple, worldly experience and common sense.

## Implications for management

Governing bodies and heads should understand their statutory duties to make policies and to publicise them. These will form the main planks for the proper use of particular sanctions in practice.

The traditional disciplinary sanctions available to teachers, detention, exclusion, physical restraint and corporal punishment are all now constrained by statutory provisions. It is important that heads and governors should understand the extent of their powers and the limits set on the exercise of the powers by teachers and other staff in the school. Heads should ensure that staff members fully understand the statutory constraints too.

The school's disciplinary policy and the types and use of sanctions in the school should be known by all staff, and should be published to parents and prospective parents in the school's prospectus.

Heads also have a duty to draw attention to the policy in the school at least once per year.

In investigations, heads and governing bodies must establish right from the beginning of a case what the factual issues are that have to be resolved, and determine from these what inquiries are necessary. These inquiries must be reasonable, and are most likely to be proactive given the responsibility of the head to get to the bottom of the issue and to make a decision. According to the Solihull case, the head has an obligation to 'ask the right question'.

In making disciplinary decisions, and in particular a decision to exclude a pupil, heads should be certain that the requirements of natural justice are observed. Pupils who might be facing a school sanction are entitled to put their side of the case before the decision is taken.

## The management of exclusions

It is still vital that heads inform parents if a child under 18 is to be excluded and inform them of the length and the reasons for it. They must also be told that they have the right to make representations, and to attend a meeting where such representations can be heard.

When an exclusion is for a longer period than a day or two, the governors should arrange to meet quickly and certainly within 15 days of the exclusion. If they uphold the exclusion, the governors should consider whether the pupil needs some extra support to prepare for re-integration.

Pupils should not, according to the DfEE, remain out of school for more than 15 days without a clear plan for re-integration.

In future LEAs will have to set out, in their Behaviour Support Plans, the circumstances in which they will arrange additional education, such as home tuition.

Ministers expect exclusions of more than 15 days to be rarely used, and mainly only when more time is needed to successfully re-integrate a pupil. There is no evidence that an exclusion of a week or longer is any more likely to prevent serious misbehaviour than an exclusion of only a day or two.

Ministers also expect that where the exclusion is for more than a day or two, pupils will receive work to do at home and have it marked.

Following the 1998 Act, parents now have the right to address the governing body before the governors decide whether to confirm the exclusion decision or not. It will be more important than ever that heads prepare the school's case well, have all the relevant documentation and witness statements, and justify the decision as objectively as possible. Consistency will be important. Heads may well be asked to compare the decision taken in one case with an earlier or different decision. This has implications for the filing of information and evidence.

Before reaching a decision to exclude, heads must make reasonable and active efforts to establish the facts and to acquire relevant evidence. No evidence which is unearthed should be ignored. The initial account of the incident made by the witnesses should be recorded. The account of the identification of the alleged malefactors should be recorded, and in addition the safeguards that have been taken to ensure that the identification evidence has not been obtained by prompting. There must eventually be sufficient evidence to underpin the decision to exclude. If this is not the case then the probability is that the investigations will have been insufficient, and the decision may be overturned if challenged.

## Challenges to decisions

Parents, and pupils over 18, can complain to the governors, and to the LEA if they are dissatisfied with particular disciplinary actions. And in the case of exclusions, can go through a statutory appeal procedure. Heads should ensure that parents are aware of their rights. This is usually set out in the prospectus, but it helps to repeat this when complaints are in the offing.

Issues concerning the unreasonable and illegal use of powers and discretions by councils and governing bodies can be referred to the Secretary of State. It has long been established that courts are unwilling to intervene before this procedure has run its course, or where the Secretary of State has exercised his or her discretion in a particular way, unless it can be demonstrated that the Secretary of State may not have properly directed him or herself when exercising the discretion. In most instances the issue is not one of the Secretary of State's improper or unreasonable use of a discretion, but a question of judgement. And the Court is not empowered to substitute its own judgement in judicial review proceedings.

The Secretary of State's powers have been extended by S8 of the **School Standards and Framework Act 1998**, which provides the Secretary of State with a general default power allowing him or her to intervene if satisfied that a body has failed to discharge its statutory duty to provide education at maintained schools of 'an adequate standard'. However, parties who have a sufficient interest in a breach of a statutory duty can still make applications to the Court if dissatisfied.

## Corporal punishment and justifiable restraint

Under sections 548 to 550 of the **Education Act 1996**, teachers may not use any degree of physical contact which is deliberately intended to be a punishment, or which is primarily intended to cause pain, injury or humiliation.

The **School Standards and Framework Act 1998** outlaws corporal punishment in all maintained and independent schools and for children receiving nursery education.

Section 550A has been added to the 1996 Act by the 1998 Act making clear that where necessary physical contact can be used to control or restrain pupils, so long as it is not part of any punishment.

Section 50A allows teachers and others authorised by the head to have control of pupils (e.g. midday supervisors) to use reasonable force in all circumstances to prevent a pupil from:

- committing a criminal offence;

- injuring themselves or others;
- causing damage to property (including the pupil's own);
- engaging in behaviour prejudicial to maintaining good order and discipline.

These apply whether on or off the premises when the teacher or non-teacher has lawful control of the pupils.

In addition to the provisions of S550A, everyone has a common law right to defend themselves against an assault providing they do not use a disproportionate amount of force to do so.

There is no legal definition of 'reasonable force'. It can only be considered in the context of its use. Any degree of force will be unlawful if the particular circumstances do not warrant it. In cases where it is warranted, the minimum necessary should be used. In most cases this will be a matter of simple common-sense. In a minority of cases it will be up to a court to determine whether it has gone beyond what could be reasonably expected.

**Circular 10/98: The Use of Force to Control or Restrain Pupils** gives detailed advice.

## Implications for management

Schools need to have a policy on the use of force to control or restrain pupils. The staff, teachers and non-teachers need to know what is acceptable and what is not.

Teachers also need to have a modicum of training, or periodic opportunities to consider this whole question, and specific aspects of control and restraint. Teachers are always concerned about touching pupils and need the opportunity to discuss with the management common approaches to such issues as comforting children in distress, and which children may consider any kind of contact as unwelcome because of their cultural background. Time should be set aside during training days for these kind of considerations. They should also be discussed with the governors.

Heads will need to consider any model LEA policy on the subject and also any advice on touching, holding or restraining that the LEA or governors might provide.

The school's policy should be made known to the parents.

The **case of the broken jaw** illustrates what happened before the new law was passed. In 1971 a 15 year old boy refused to get changed for a PE lesson. The PE teacher shouted at him until the boy eventually got changed, but into unsuitable gear, including 'bovver boots'. In the ensuing row the boy kicked and punched the teacher, who responded by hitting him and breaking his jaw. It was subsequently discovered that the boy had taken LSD before coming to school.

The parents complained, the teacher was suspended, and the police charged him with assault. The magistrates expressed their sorrow at having to find the teacher guilty, but did so and fined him.

The teacher appealed, and at the end the judge memorably asked the rhetorical question, "Have we really reached the stage in this country when an insolent and bolshie pupil has to be treated with all the courtesies of visiting royalty?"

He went on to say that a teacher does not have to have the patience of a saint. The boy was guilty of numerous offences for which he could have been convicted in a juvenile court, while it was the teacher, who was of exemplary character, who had been brought before the Court. He was acquitted. **R v Higgitt 1972**.

There are other cases where courts have shown similar understanding of the predicament that teachers can find themselves in when faced with extreme provocation on single occasions. But where there is a history of violent reaction teachers have been summarily dismissed.

At one disciplinary hearing a governing body lifted a teacher's suspension after he had been accused of hitting a pupil, even though a group of pupils testified to seeing the incident. It was sufficient for the governors that some of the pupils could not agree the details, and in the event of the uncertainty they were advised to reinstate the teacher.

# INDEX